Key Debates in Education

Available from Continuum:

John Beck and Mary Earl: *Key Issues in Secondary Education*
Asher Cashdan and Lyn Overall: *Teaching in Primary Schools*
Catherine Matheson and David Matheson: *Educational Issues in the Learning Age*
Mark O'Hara: *Teaching 3–8*
John Wilson: *Key Issues in Education and Teaching*

KEY DEBATES IN EDUCATION

Ian Davies, Ian Gregory and Nicholas McGuinn

continuum
LONDON • NEW YORK

Continuum
The Tower Building   370 Lexington Avenue
11 York Road   New York
London SE1 7NX   NY 10017-6503

© 2002 Ian Davies, Ian Gregory, Nicholas McGuinn

First published 2002

British Library Cataloguing-in-Publication Data
A catalogue record for this book is available from the British Library.

ISBN: 0-8264-5805-X (hardback) 0-8264-5128-4 (paperback)

Typeset by CentraServe Ltd, Saffron Walden, Essex
Printed and bound in Great Britain by MPG Books Ltd, Bodmin, Cornwall

Contents

Acknowledgements

This book ranges over many different issues and includes many ideas, arguments and some factual information. As a result the authors wish to acknowledge the very valuable inputs made by many people throughout our professional careers. It would perhaps be invidious to name some individuals and not others as being at least partly responsible for the development of our thinking and for providing opportunities to gain professional experience. We do hope, however, that all of our current and past students and colleagues will recognize some of the debates that have been included in this book and their contributions. We are grateful to them for their encouragement and insights and we hope that this general message of thanks is sufficient.

More particular thanks can be given to those individuals who have completed specific tasks during the time this book was being written. Professor Alan McClelland was kind enough to share his expertise in the development of the 'Very Brief History of Education' (see the appendix). Anthony Haynes was, as always, a positive and skilful editor.

Hannah, Matthew and Rachael Davies were always supportive and helped me to think about the education they are currently receiving. Lynn Davies has discussed with me many educational ideas over the past twenty years. She has often been responsible for raising new issues, relating ideas to practical school contexts and, in very many ways, providing meaning to what is debated in this book.

Ian Davies, May 2001

Essential Debates in Education: An Introduction

Ian Davies, Ian Gregory and Nick McGuinn

What Is This Book About?

This book is an introductory text that discusses some of the key issues that are significant at the moment for how we *think* about education. It also explores what we currently *do* to help people become better educated.

The purpose of the book is to encourage greater insight into issues that matter. In order to do this, the authors debate some issues and hope that our readers will become involved, as they read, in ongoing arguments. The process of those debates shown in the various chapters should lead to readers developing both greater understanding and a better ability to become involved.

Who Should Read This Book?

This book is written for all those who have a serious and sustained interest in education. Everyone is, to use the current jargon, a 'stakeholder' in education. So much of what we do is strongly related to education that indirect involvement in the issues that are debated in this book is total. No-one is unaffected. The government invests hugely in education, arguing that a successful economy depends on it. Personal involvement is also very significant. We have all been educated in one way or another. Many of us continue to be directly involved in educational institutions as teachers and learners. It is easy to argue that we all should know a little more about this vast educational enterprise that affects our daily lives in many ways. And yet, this book also has a very specific audience. In recent years there has been a very dramatic increase in the number of students in institutions of higher education who are investigating educational issues. This book will be of relevance to graduates but it is specifically targeted at undergraduates who are reading Education. If you are one of those students you should know that you are part of a growing group. There are now over 60 institutions in the UK alone offering undergraduate courses in Education with nearly half of that number offering single honours degree courses in Educational Studies. This book is meant principally for those students. We have reviewed much of the published information to ensure that as far as possible this book will be of direct benefit to you if you are following one of those courses. What is true of the UK is also true of Australia, North America and elsewhere. Programmes geared to a series of modules on core issues in education can be seen worldwide. These universities all encourage a study of these issues in a way that relates very closely to the chapter headings in this book. There is an emphasis on the aims and purposes of education, issues to do with understanding teaching and learning, the importance of understanding the shaping of policy, developing a sense of the range of responsibilities falling to education and so on. It would be too much to claim that this book will help you to understand all the issues that undergraduates studying Education will meet during their academic work but we are, of course, hoping that at least some of the complexities that surround education will become a little less difficult after reading this book.

What Is in the Book?

As well as this introduction, there are five main chapters and a conclusion. The five chapters are themselves divided into three parts: a main statement, a somewhat shorter response to that statement and a series of suggested activities and further reading that should help to develop further your understanding of particular issues. More will be said later in this introduction about the rationale for this structure. At this point it is sufficient to make clear in a general and fairly straightforward manner what the chapters contain. This description of what is contained in the book will also provide an acknowledgement that in our short space we are not promising to cover all perspectives. We do not explore all analytical perspectives (for example, there is no real discussion of vital debates arising from feminism). There is no detailed discussion about all curriculum areas (for example, mathematics education is not investigated separately). We refer largely to developments within England. We have merely tried to cover some of the areas that we feel are important in a fairly general way.

The main part of the book begins with a fundamental overview of the nature of the aims of education. Chapter 1 (The Aims of Education) sets the scene of much of what follows. If we are serious about our intention to understand and promote debate about education then we should know at least a little about the nature of the central purposes. In this chapter a number of key issues are probed. What really is the value of education? Do we agree about the role of education? Is it something that should focus on better academic thinking or are there other targets and priorities? What is the difference between education and schooling?

In Chapter 2 the meaning of learning is considered. This chapter has obvious importance. If schools are not places where learning takes place then they perhaps cannot be justified. This seemingly simple point does need to be remembered in light of the debates (also represented in this book) about, for example, the political and economic contexts of schooling. Psychological aspects of what is learnt and how it is learnt are at the heart of this chapter. It considers various motivations that might assist learning, referring to the tensions between 'transmissive' (telling) and 'dialogic' approaches (discussing and negotiating); and differences of learning style and what has been called 'multiple intelligences'.

Chapter 3 complements, in some ways, the discussion that took place in Chapter 2. There are further thoughts in Chapter 3 about learning and also teaching, but two new elements appear. Assessment is given major attention. Should we assess children's understanding? Some would argue that assessment is unavoidable in any social situation. If this is right then what should be assessed and how? What are the alternatives: not only to assessment but perhaps to school itself? Do we really have a number of viable different approaches or should we bow to the inevitable and accept a version of schooling that is rather similar to what we already have?

Chapter 4 explores educational policy-making. The great changes to our education system in the last twenty years are considered with a particular focus on legal matters. The increased emphasis on the perceived need for schools to be more accountable is discussed. Identifying the gaps between the ambitions of policy and the emerging reality is a good way of highlighting some very significant matters. Does the state always need to organize education systems? Should school be compulsory? These questions will seem to some to lead to obvious answers and yet the close focus on policy-making and implementation in this chapter allows for a greater appreciation of the complexities of educational policies in the contemporary world.

Chapter 5 asks, provocatively, questions about the notion of 'education for a better world'. There has always been a tremendously strong assertion made by many that education has the power to transform. At times this change has been limited. Schools, for example, have merely been the buildings through which benefits such as free school meals or health care checks have been channelled. At other times there is something about the substance of what is being taught and learnt that means it is possible for individuals and communities to know themselves better and to be able to make things better for others. Currently citizenship education is very high on the national and international agenda and this relates strongly to some of the issues raised here. Chapter 5 raises arguments and poses questions about the variety of initiatives that characterize education as a social project.

The conclusions to the book are not merely a summary of comments that have been made earlier in the book. Rather, we want to provide a way of allowing readers to think about the meaning of education and how it develops. We provide a series of brief biographies of people who we have referred to as 'great educators'. These people have made, in one way or another, major contributions to the thinking or practice of education. We provide some factual information as historical background and, by so doing, locate them in a particular set of circumstances. We also summarize and comment upon their work to show what made them special. We also provide an overview of the nature of a great educator. If we know who these people are and what they have done, and understand the nature of their contribution then we will have opportunities to make contemporary work on education less free floating than it sometimes appears. Of course we are not claiming that we have identified the list of great educators that everyone would mention. We apologize if your 'favourite' has been omitted. Neither do we suggest that our summaries or interpretations of their work are not open to question. You may find other and better ways of coming to understand education. We definitely do not want to suggest that better education is made by individuals who for the most part are, like most people that we have in our list of 'great educators', white, male and dead. Nor, finally, do we suggest that we will have a very clear and straightforward path to making improvements in our thinking or practical applications of educational work merely by having a better understanding of a few key individuals. We do, however, suggest that there is some point in knowing what has gone before so that a more informed, reflective and thorough consideration can be developed.

How Should This Book Be Read?

This question needs to be considered very carefully for this is not the sort of book that is written by 'experts' for 'novices'. Of course, we hope that after many years of work in a wide variety of educational institutions we, the authors, have something to offer people who have not had so much experience. We do not think that knowledge is unnecessary, nor do we think that all views have equal value. Some ideas are simply better, and, at times, better expressed, than others. However, the principal aims of this book are to display a debate between the authors and to encourage the readers to enter into this creative conflict. We will not be able to hear you shouting at the pages – cheering or sneering – but we *do* want to provoke responses. The intended main audience (those fairly new to the study and practice of education) and the determination to generate responses from readers has led to the use of a particular style. This style is one that we hope will make the readers feel as if they are part of lively controversial debates about things that matter. We aim to be provocative. Of course, none of the authors has fabricated any of the material. We are not saying things we do not believe. But some of the comments are at times a little overstated for effect and there may be occasions when – for reasons of space, time and the need to make things as accessible as possible – we may have erred into the sort of comment that we may later regret. But that is the nature of debate and we hope that the readers will accept the contributions with this in mind.

The book has been constructed around a framework that will allow for debate. It has been written by a team of three people who argue against each other. Each chapter begins with a main statement by one author. The single author responsible for the main statement in a chapter uses, generally, specialist knowledge that the other two authors do not have. Nevertheless, one of the remaining two authors has supplied an individual response to each of the main statements. The responses are meant to highlight key issues and our differences. Each chapter finishes with a list of key questions, suggestions for further reading and activities. These activities are largely based on an awareness of the issues that the respondents felt it was important to pursue. So, for example, Ian Gregory, drawing on his work as a philosopher of education, has written Chapter 1 on educational aims; Ian Davies wrote the response to that chapter; Ian Gregory then wrote a series of activities and supplied some suggestions for further reading.

To be able to make some sort of sense of what our arguments mean, it will probably be useful if the reader knows a little about our backgrounds and main ideas. Of course, we do not want the reader to think that there is a necessary causal link between experience and the formation of particular opinions. We also should admit that we do not perceive huge ideological differences between ourselves. We are in many ways rather similar people who work together and get along very well with each other. And yet, it is in these circumstances that real debate can occur. We did not want to write a book that contained chapters written by people who have, supposedly, diametrically opposed views. Television interviewers are surely wrong when they manage debates as some sort of gladiatorial conflict in which the whole point of the exercise is to score points rather than to develop a meaningful exploration of difficult and important issues. The bulk of serious debate about education today is not, whatever the tabloid press might suggest, between violently opposed extremists. Rather, the nuances and subtleties of arguments need to be examined and this is best illustrated by listening to debates involving people who hold much in common. It is only in this way that we can get beyond rather meaningless generalities or slanging matches where there is no common ground. But the common ground between us contains significant breaks. We do not feel that we are merely broadcasting petty disputes. We wish to avoid (in Freud's telling phrase) the 'narcissism of small differences' and get to the heart of matters. We are all in favour of a good educational system that works well for all those involved, but what does that really mean? We need to encourage readers to see the differences that really emerge when well-meaning people try to argue for better ideas and practice in education.

We hope that the following details about the authors' professional experiences and views supply a limited context for the chapters that follow and make our debates easier to follow. It is probably best in these circumstances to avoid too much pseudo psychoanalytical navel-gazing. The wailings of the 'me generation' have been heard enough already. We do not want too much sentiment. And yet, perhaps a little background information (in the authors' own words) will allow the reader to cast a critical eye over the statements and responses we make in this book. In short, the reader should know where we are 'coming from'.

The Authors

Ian Davies: I have worked at the University of York since 1989. Prior to that I was a teacher in comprehensive schools in England for ten years. I have longstanding interests in history education and citizenship education. The roots of these interests are hard to identify. I passed the '11-plus' and went to a boys' state grammar school in Liverpool. (The '11-plus' was the main way in which young people, at age 11, were sorted into schools that were supposed to suit their aptitudes and abilities. Failure in the, rather unreliable, examination would normally lead to entry to a secondary modern school which was supposed in theory to be of equal status.) Today, issues to do with social class and education are rather neglected but, at least at that time (the 1960s), I suppose my background is what used to be described as 'working class'. A very good teacher (Maurice Devereux) inspired me to become interested in history. I think I always had strong interests in politics. Liverpool has always seemed a very politicized city and debates at home within the family sharpened my interests. I became an undergraduate at York in the 1970s just at the time when ideas to do with political education were being developed. My career ambitions had been either social work or teaching. I eventually followed the route of so many people from my background and decided that I wanted to work with young people who were in mainstream schools. My initial teacher education course included a placement at the Abraham Moss Community School in Manchester. At the time (the late 1970s) Abraham Moss was a very high-profile institution which saw its role not only as a school but also as a body that could stimulate and work together with local and other communities. I went on to teach mainly history in comprehensive schools in Grimsby and Andover and to being involved in the shift from providing a fact-based narrative to the 'new history' that more explicitly stimulated skills-based learning. Throughout my teaching career I was taking deliberate decisions not to work in grammar or private schools. I am sure that I displayed plenty of naïve youthful idealism but I do feel privileged to have worked with some excellent teachers and do feel very positive indeed about the work that goes on in schools. When I moved to work at the University of York in 1989, from a role as head of humanities, it was in some ways prompted by a desire to keep in touch with schools and teaching rather than to move towards the next 'obvious' step of being embroiled in the administrative demands of being a deputy head. My work with teachers and those who are working to gain qualified teacher status is hugely rewarding. That said, I do at times feel some doubts about my present position within a selective higher education system that is some way removed from the 'chalk face'. A deeply felt desire to educate people about contemporary society is still what I like to think I am 'about'. I would also like to think that I help people to think about (and perhaps do something about) how to make society a little better. Thus, education for me has always been a social project. Its purpose is not necessarily or principally to do with personal growth or individual cognitive acceleration. It is more about a desire to study society, think critically and to provide an education that helps people develop their potential to improve things. As such, education has for me a strong utilitarian function. To state my position in a simplistic way, I see education as being less about individuals achieving 'glittering prizes' and more about raising standards appropriately to allow for the possibility of societal improvement. The arguments over the nature of the preferred outcome is, for me, the key debate in education. But that debate does, I believe, have certain parameters. While there must be space for individual professional creativity – this is what good teaching (indeed, a good society) is all about – it is necessary for agreements to be reached about what all should have access and entitlements to. As such, commitment to broad principles such as equality are important. The extent to which particular strategies can be seen as necessary is problematic and can only be reviewed on a case-by-case basis. Nevertheless I do think that policies such as the National Curriculum, for example, can, if approached in certain ways, provide very positive ways forward.

Ian Gregory: I think I enjoyed a good education. I went to a good Catholic primary school; I transferred to a very good Catholic grammar school in the south of England, being one of those lucky ones who passed the 11-plus. Someone like myself acts as a justification for those who clamour for the return of something very like the 11-plus nowadays or who resist its abolition in those areas where it still exists. I was a young child from a relatively deprived background with ability who the 11-plus picked out as someone deserving of an appropriate education. Without a mechanism like the 11-plus, I might have sunk without trace if the only kind of education on offer was non-selective (so the story goes).

I subsequently went to university in London and Oxford where I studied philosophy. At a later stage in my life while working at the University of York I studied for a law degree part time at the University of Hull. Apart from a brief period working in a library and sundry part-time jobs such as greenkeeping, cutting the grass for the local council and working in the cold store of an ice cream factory, I have spent my life working in universities. My academic specialities are, unsurprisingly, philosophy and law. And overwhelmingly I have plied those trades in departments of education.

Those are the bare bones of my intellectual history. My philosophical education was in the very heyday of linguistic philosophy. I think of philosophy as analytical, as essentially a critical and clarificatory activity. This tradition of philosophizing is the scourge of obscurity, dogmatism and slippery argument. It insists upon the careful use of language, it lays bare the presuppositions of arguments, it explores their implications, and it vets them for coherence and consistency. We should always be on our guard against the intellectually shoddy. So why apply philosophy to the concerns of education? Education is one of the great human enterprises – perhaps the greatest. What could be more important? It is, however, one of those areas (rather like the domain of party politics) where the quality of debate is characteristically feeble, where in the drive to carry conviction confused language and argument seeks to by-pass our critical faculties. Too much educational discourse is, as R. S. Peters puts it, 'undifferentiated mush'. It is my distaste for such mush that persuades me that thinking critically and clearly about educational matters is of the most profound importance. Critical debate about such matters must be kept alive, especially so it seems to me at the present time, where central government exhibits such a displeasing certainty as to the way forward for the nation's schools.

My other great interest is education law. In the last twenty years this area has burgeoned. It is no longer the dormant area of law of the previous 40 years subsequent to 1944 (the date when the Butler Education Act became law – see the appendix for details). Education law is the barometer and expression of government policy in the key area of education. I find myself deeply unsympathetic to the thrust of government policies of the last twenty years, whether those of the Conservatives or more latterly the Labour Party. There have, of course, been intellectual influences that have shaped my outlook – the deschoolers and the children rights movement in particular spring to mind. But it has been the experience of my own children's schooling that has influenced me more than anything else. All comparison between their education and my own was to the detriment of my own schooling. They went to the local primary school and the local rural comprehensive. I was continually struck by the self-confidence they exhibited in their writings, the opportunities they enjoyed to take responsibility for their own learning, the humane nature of teacher–pupil relationships, their much greater enjoyment of schooling than I ever knew. All of this I saw at first hand as a governor of the secondary school. They have all thrived academically because of the confidence their schooling inspired in them.

By contrast the sheer dullness of my own education, however 'good', was made palpable to me. It is a source of immense pleasure to me that my children finished their schooling before the dead hand of the National Curriculum (provided for in the Education Reform Act of 1988), and everything that came in its wake, was implemented fully. I fear for the future of schooling as the tentacles of the state spread to every nook and cranny of school life. The humane impulses that flowed through the schooling system in the sixties and seventies are in danger of being swept away. That a liberal society has allowed government the degree of control it presently enjoys over the nation's schooling is deeply depressing and to be deplored.

Nick McGuinn: From the day when I was dragged, protesting, out of the nursery sandpit and into the reception classroom of my primary school, education has played a major part in my life. I have been on the receiving-end of many different teaching styles since then: some of them inspirational, some not so impressive. I have been enthralled by a skilful sixth-form teacher's ability to explicate Shakespeare's *King Lear* line by line, and I have quaked with fear as a maths teacher has threatened a beating if I failed to answer a mental arithmetic question.

It was a Jesuit priest who famously said, 'Give me the child till the age of seven, and I will give you the man.' I passed into the care of this particular Catholic order when I was double that recommended age. Whether this meant it was too late for the fathers to make their mark on me, I can't say. I remember a great deal of preaching about hell-fire; but I remember, too, much emphasis upon concepts of responsibility and community.

Perhaps this links to the particular period – the sixties and early seventies – when I attended school and university. This was a time when belief in the transformational power of education – even education for its own sake – ran strong. I still remain deeply impressed by the fact that I lived through a period when taxpayers were prepared to finance students like myself to study English Literature – in my case the novels of George Eliot – to higher degree level without any expectation of repayment. If it did me good, the thinking seemed to be, it might somehow do the community good as well.

I think this was a fruitful approach. Many young people of my generation left university with a strong feeling that they needed to give something back to society. Instead of looking for lucrative jobs in advertising and the media – which are now, I understand, the preferred options of many English graduates – we turned to the 'caring' professions like teaching. So I completed my years at Oxford with a postgraduate certificate in education. It was an interesting time to enter the profession. The Labour Government of the day had recently committed itself to the comprehensive school. The Bullock Report (developed in the1970s) on the teaching of English had reinvigorated English teaching. The establishment I joined as a newly qualified teacher in 1977 seemed to be right at the heart of things. It was a newly formed comprehensive, based on the amalgamation of three schools: a primary, a secondary modern and a grammar. It contained 2000 pupils of widely different aspirations, backgrounds and abilities, with all the challenges and underlying tensions that might imply.

What motivated young English teachers like myself in those days? A desire to share our love of literature, yes; but we also wanted to help each of our pupils find their own personal voice, to negotiate their sense of being in the world, through the medium of language. And now that I am in danger of sounding pretentious, I may as well go further and suggest that we also believed, deeply, in the idea that increasingly fragmented communities could be brought together through the medium of the shared cultural experience. In this respect drama – so lacking from my own education – proved a revelation to me. I was amazed to see how dramatic techniques could change the power relationship of teacher and learner, conferring the 'mantle of the expert' upon the latter and helping often hesitant and unconfident young people find a voice and a purpose within the safety of the fictional drama space.

Much of our pedagogical approach was grounded in a philosophy of English teaching which reached back through the years via Bullock, F. R. Leavis (literary critic active 1930s to 1970s) and the Newbolt Report of 1921 into the teaching of English, to Matthew

Arnold (poet and schools inspector of the nineteenth century) and perhaps even further, to the poet and critic Samuel Taylor Coleridge in the early nineteenth century. It was a pedagogy which believed in the power of culture to nourish the spirit and the community and thus offer a defence against the encroaching forces of materialism and mass-manipulation.

One did not have to be teaching long to realize that such an approach just would not do. English is spoken by many different voices and each has its own pressing concerns. When the National Curriculum was introduced in 1988, the Working Party for English tried to identify and draw together its different strands. Yes, there was a place for the transmission of the 'cultural heritage' and the nurturing of 'personal growth'; but there was also a requirement – in a world where the demands of literacy were growing ever more complex and challenging – for 'cultural analysis', 'adult needs' and 'language across the curriculum'.

New genres of spoken and written language began to enter the classroom. We learnt to accommodate the claims of non-fiction, of media texts, of accents and dialects and varieties of English which had not previously been granted their due. This in turn brought a new focus upon the structures of language at text, sentence and word level. New pressures arose: how might it be possible to address such a broad range of subject knowledge, skills and understanding within the ambit of 'English'? What room remained for concerns about the personal voice or about personal growth?

The coherence of our subject has been challenged even further by the advent of literary theories which, by moving the focus of interpretation from writer to reader, have replaced the idea of a unifying vision with one of multiple viewpoints and realities. The technological revolution has changed utterly the way we think about text and authorship and communication. While the boundaries of English are being pushed ever further by developments such as these, so there is a counteracting political pressure (usually emanating from the Right) to use the subject as a means of re-establishing former certainties of identity and purpose against the perceived threat of moral and cultural relativism.

So that is where I am today, 24 years after teaching my first lesson in that 2000-strong comprehensive school. I still go back to it, not to teach this time, but to watch young students learn our difficult trade. In this book, I'm the one who keeps grounding my educational ideas in imaginative literature and who is still trying to answer the question: How do we balance the needs and claims of the personal voice with the demands of the society within which that voice must speak and be heard?

What are the Key Issues in Education Today?

Everyone is an educational expert and education itself is held up as the universal panacea. But just what is education? At least three formulations are used when it is discussed. First, there is the sense in which education is seen as something that you receive as a token of success. When it is said: 'She is well educated', we often take it to mean that that person has passed a number of examinations. In other words the person is well qualified. Whether or not they are automatically to be regarded as intelligent or well educated in a broader sense is sometimes assumed but is normally not clear. Secondly, education can refer to the content of what is taught and the processes of learning in schools and colleges. This is fiercely debated. These discussions, as we suggest below, can be viewed from a variety of perspectives. Thirdly, there is a rigorous, and fairly new, study of education. The three authors of this book work within a department of educational studies. Academic subjects come and go. The study of Latin has declined, and it seems as if we are experiencing the rise of Educational Studies. It is perhaps worth exploring, even if only superficially, why this growth has occurred. Education is recognized as a vitally important area of contemporary life. Not to study it would be to disregard massive economic and human investment. It is vitally significant to all our lives and we need to understand it better. There are however, other less comfortable reasons for the growth of Educational Studies. As higher education expands and 'customers' are allowed to choose what to study, there are opportunities for new areas to find their way on to the curriculum. There are particular opportunities for universities to move into this expanding market as so much of teacher education has been shifted away from the universities and into the schools. As the power of the 'educational establishment' (local education authorities, university departments of education and Her Majesty's Inspectorate) have withered, leaving teacher education to others, Educational Studies rises Phoenix-like from the ashes. This new creation does not give students qualified teacher status but it does promote critical thought about the educational system that brought it into being.

The sort of issues and trends that are studied in these university programmes of Educational Studies vary, as one might expect, hugely. Education is perhaps not yet an academic discipline in its own right but more of an area of study that uses established ways of thinking for its own purposes. Two obvious contexts for study are politics and economics. A study of the politics of education could involve an examination of the development of educational policy, the meaning of education in political contexts and the debates over the differences between 'genuine' learning and 'mere' socialization. The economics of education is an important field in which students have the opportunity to see both society investing in education, and students and others in the role of consumers. More specific contexts beyond broad areas of politics and economics would include a huge range of issues including special educational needs, learning particular subjects (drawing largely from the psychology of education) and comparative education. Less context bound and more related to academic disciplines are those degree programmes and modules that, for example, focus on philosophy of education or sociology.

The history of education is clearly another important area. Students do not seem greatly entranced by lists of dates, names of long-dead politicians and accounts of 'significant' educational legislation. However, the historical trends that illustrate the nature of educational development can be of interest. The appendix gives a bald summary of some key dates but what are the broad headlines for the last century? Some would argue that the debates have moved from interlocking arguments over *access* through *process* to *standards*. As the state education system grew (and we should not forget its relatively recent origin, becoming compulsory only in 1880), the first matter was to get people involved. This became at first a general struggle over the need to improve attendance figures and to raise the school leaving age, and then moved to a consideration of particular excluded groups (the working class, girls, black pupils). Process became very important when it was felt that being present in school was not enough. It was felt for a time that the *means* by which you were educated said a good deal more about what you learnt than anything else. Experiential learning, the hidden curriculum and making education relevant, often to the whole person rather than just the brain, became the driving force for some people from the 1960s onwards. 'Standards', however, seems to be the current watchword. Although there are obviously huge overlaps with the other debates mentioned here, we are now more ready to assume that most pupils will attend and that we will use whatever method is necessary to ensure that they learn something. The debates over structures (although still very keenly felt with recent moves to specialist schools) are far less angry than the old debates over comprehensive and grammar schools. We are now locked into a clearer and more obviously utilitarian stance in which basic skills and examination passes are the signs of success. Curriculum choices can, of course, still be made. There are preferences for cognitive or affective education. There are debates about the extent to which we should focus pupils' minds on what we deem useful for today's world or whether a more general capacity to think and be autonomous should be our priority. But education today appears less contentious than it once was. The government knows what it wants and does not mind telling teachers what it thinks. The 'secret garden' of the curriculum, in which only the educational professionals were allowed entry, lasted until the 1970s and has now gone. The Labour minister who declared proudly in the 1940s that 'the minister knows "nowt" about curriculum' would not last for long today. This may be no bad thing.

What do the above points signify? The purpose of this book is not for the authors to tell you what to think. It is rather to outline a few of the thousands of arguments about education and to invite the reader to join this most vital and essentially contested of debates.

CHAPTER 1

The Aims of Education

Ian Gregory

Preliminaries

Individuals go into teaching for all kind of reasons. They like children, their parents are teachers, and the thought of all those school holidays attracts them. Perhaps they want a career that, while offering them less in the way of material reward, offers the prospect of continuing employment – after all society always needs teachers. They might be tempted by the thought that as a teacher they have a certain status within society. And maybe (just maybe!) the financial prospects of a career in teaching look tempting and fuel ambition to do well in their chosen career. Some cynics have even suggested that many go into teaching just because they dislike children and a life in teaching affords limitless opportunities to give vent to that dislike. It is possible to go on and on speculating on the motivations that lead individuals to become teachers. What is certain is that many would respond to the query 'Why did you become a teacher?' that they think education is important and that they wish to help educate the young in just the same way that a previous generation of teachers brought them to enjoy the benefits of education.

The foregoing observations, banal though they are, highlight some important facts about education in any society with which readers of this book are familiar. In the main, the provision of education is not left to chance. There are professionals called teachers who take it upon themselves to promote the education of the young and for which task they are employed. They pass their professional lives in educational institutions – schools, colleges of further education, institutions of higher education. In saying the education of the young is not left to chance we are saying that education is provided as part of a systematic purposive effort to educate the young. We (society) take it upon ourselves to ensure that all young people enjoy an education because we think education is immensely important, both for the individual concerned but also for the wider society within which individuals will pass their lives. In our times, we emphasize our sense of just how important education is to the flourishing and welfare of the young by proclaiming education as one of the fundamental human rights. In so putting it, we express the profound conviction that for the young not to enjoy access to an education is to be harmed, for them to be deliberately denied an education is a great moral wrong.

Governments see the delivery of high quality education to their young as being of paramount importance. If a central government comes to think that its education service is failing its young, education becomes a major political concern. The enormous investment of government time, energy and resource into our own education service in England and Wales, and elsewhere, is both a testimony to the sense that the provision of education is seen as of primary social importance as well as giving expression to the sense that what is being delivered is (sometimes) not of sufficient quality and, in keeping with its importance, must be improved. Given that teachers are (as things are presently arranged) key to successful education we should not be surprised that they find themselves in the firing line of government initiatives.

This emphasis upon the importance of education is commonplace. But what might not be so obvious is why education is so important and how *fundamental* is the importance of education as a distinctively *human* enterprise. It is in the effort to spell out what its importance consists in that talk about the aims of education enjoys its significance. There are some questions that demand our attention and which we never seem able to finally turn our back on. Among such questions is our interest in the (proper) aims of education. The history of educational thought is replete with efforts to persuade us what education should take as its key aims and purposes. A conventional list of so-called 'great educators' – Plato, Quintilian, Comenius, Locke, Rousseau, Pestalozzi, Froebel, Montessori and Dewey, to mention only a few – have all presented us with visions of education and its possibilities designed to persuade us as to the proper purposes and ends of education and how it should be conducted. One way of representing their efforts in this area is to talk of their respective 'philosophies of education'. It is common to talk of 'educational theorists' or 'philosophers of education' but for the sake of clarity it is well worth drawing attention to the distinction between 'The Philosophy of Education' as *an activity* and the philosophies of education associated with our educational theorists. The former takes as (part of) its subject matter those philosophies of education, their concepts and principles and seeks to understand the nature of the activity represented by the construction of such educational theories. Its ambitions are *clarificatory* rather than driven by the desire to get us to act in ways recommended and inspired by any educational theorist's 'philosophy of education'.

The single most influential figure in 'The Philosophy of Education' since the 1960s is without doubt R. S. Peters, author of *Ethics and Education* (1966), arguably the text that gave substance (and a measure of respectability also) to the rather indeterminate field of 'The Philosophy of Education'. His initial concern was fuelled by his recognition that at the time there existed little in the way of a critical and analytical literature around the concept of education and associated notions. Talk and discussion about education lacked clarity and rigour and was too inspired by the enthusiasms of those who sought to bring about the changes in educational practice they deemed desirable. In the natural desire to effect change, reason was being left out of the equation. Peters memorably re-invoked the metaphor of too much educational discourse being a kind of 'undifferentiated mush' – difficult to make sense of and assess because of its too often desperate obscurity. Within this context was born 'The Philosophy of Education' as an enterprise using the techniques and tools of the analytical philosophy of the time to clarify and sharpen our appreciation of educational terms and concepts, argument and debate. This chapter is driven by just such an ambition while at the same time recognizing that while clarity is important, it is not everything. Especially in education which above all seeks to make a difference both to individuals and society.

Education: Some Conceptual Mapping

Inspired by Peters's example it will be helpful to remind ourselves of the variety of ways in which we utilize the concept of education and how pervasive such talk is.

Education is something that is provided, sought out and largely insisted upon by most states for their young. It is provided through a whole variety of institutions embracing the entire age range from the very young through to adults of any age, pursuing further (or, sometimes, for what seems the first time) opportunities of education. There is a bewildering variety of educational systems charged with delivering education to a nation's peoples. These systems reflect different cultural patterns, nations' different histories, different religious traditions, different forms of government and so on. The ability of a nation to deliver education to its people will probably reflect its economic strength. The so-called economically developed nations as a matter of course make provision for educational opportunities from pre-school days through to higher education. Many of the poorer nations struggle to provide even the rudiments of primary education for the very young. Where this is so, we wish it could be otherwise.

The emphasis upon provision is important. It is a demonstration that whether it must be so or not, education and its delivery is something systematically and purposively pursued. The symbols of this purposive activity are schools and institutions of further and higher education. There is a key distinction to be drawn between education and *schooling*, the vehicle through which we seek, in the main, to realize our educational goals and purposes. The activity (or task) of education is laid upon schools. They are judged as being more or less successful at that task. Whatever our ambitions are in educating the young, schools (for reasons bound up with the kinds of institutions they are) might not be as successful as we would like. We need to remind ourselves that schools might well serve purposes that owe little to education and its aims. The outcomes of schooling and education are not necessarily coincidental. In short, schooling and education are not the same, even if schools can (and do) go some way to realizing our educational ambitions. Perhaps we should listen to those like Illich, Freire, Holt and Goodman, who in varying ways argue that if the ends of education are to be best served, we need to encourage education outside of the school context. Be that as it may, the concept of education must not be confused with the idea of schooling. The notion of being *self-educated* not only makes perfect sense, but the reality is that there exist large numbers of such persons who by dint of their own efforts have compensated for what schools (and other educational institutions) have failed to deliver. The distinction between *formal* education and *informal* education is surely well taken as is the phenomenon of *lifelong education* realized either through formal educational provision or more informal methods.

We talk of people being ill educated, barely educated, half educated and lacking in education. We talk of individuals being educated, well educated, very well educated, of having enjoyed a good education, being educable, and the limiting instance of being ineducable. These ways of talking suggest individuals who to varying degrees enjoy or lack something deemed to be of value or who have or lack the capacity to enjoy the benefit of education. In the ordinary course of events, we do not dissent from the proposition that providing individuals with an education is a good thing or that it is better (a more desirable state of affairs) to be educated than not. What is involved in these sentiments needs to be understood more clearly.

The enterprise of education can be delivered under so many different categories. Talk abounds of: aesthetic education, scientific education, moral education, literary education, mathematical education, legal education, religious education, physical education, political and social education, anti-racist education, anti-sexist education, education for the post-modern world, education for democracy, education of the emotions and the like. We even hear talk such as 'my footballing education was completed by a period of time with Arsenal in the 1980s'. This and similar claims can be, and are, made in respect of almost any activity with which human beings can be associated. We need to understand (again) more clearly what might be involved in such ways of talking.

To complete this very untidy and rather disparate trawl of the language of education, we distinguish between education and phenomena such as acculturation, socialization, adaptation, habituation training, indoctrination, conditioning. Whatever the final differences between these bedrock concepts that relate to the accommodation of humans with the social world within which they have to pass their lives, it is surely worth presuming (unless there are very compelling reasons to come to doubt it) that these different words (and concepts) reflect real differences in ways of shaping human consciousness – differences which should be borne in mind if confusion is to be avoided.

No doubt with sufficient time and effort a rich and very complex mapping of the conceptual geography of education and its cognates could be generated. But, why bother? The concluding comment of the last paragraph holds the key. Wittgenstein has made us familiar with the idea of language as a tool we humans use to serve our purposes. Distinctions we find it helpful to mark are captured by the words with which we operate. The distinctions we draw, we draw precisely because we recognize and feel the need to recognize linguistically differences that have seemed to us to be of importance. The implication of this is clear: the fact we have a word 'education' and another word (say) 'indoctrination' suggests that these words (standing as the linguistic representation of the underlying concepts) mean different things and pick out different aspects of our social reality. And what is true of these two words applies in full measure to education and so many of those other words like 'socialization' and the like. The philosophical task is to make plain to us something of the nature of those differences and how and why, where there is confusion about such matters, confusion is possible. But that will only be possible if we are able to say something of a more general nature about the very idea of 'education'.

More on 'Education'

Enough has been done to alert us to the variety of uses and contexts involving education and its cognates. Our ultimate ambition is to cast some light upon talk about the aims of education. It seems unlikely we can progress very far down that path without some grasp of the most distinctive features of education. But we should not expect any very startling revelations as to what those features are. It would be very surprising if a term (notion, idea, concept) enjoying such wide currency, and which is used with such confidence and certainty most of the time, was mysterious in its significance. Given, however, the very wide currency of its use we should give up on any ambition we might have to capture its essential meaning in some quick definition which will capture and explain its use in all those very different contexts in which it is used. Rather we should hope to see talk of education in all of its guises against the background of other notions, which notions typically are to be invoked when there is talk of education. We should lay down 'parameters of intelligibility' which govern discourse about education. It should be possible to say something about education which is descriptive of the concept. It is sometimes argued to the contrary that the distinction between *concept description* and *concept construction* is not possible to draw in the case of education. That is, any ostensibly descriptive account of what education is *must* smuggle in (be the expression of) certain preferences of a moral, social or political kind that education is designed to serve. In this area, the distinction between the *descriptive* and the *evaluative* is not able to be sustained.

There is no reason to doubt that definition *has* been used to persuade others to come to share a vision of what education *should* be about. *Persuasive definitions* as such definitions have been called abound in educational discourse and theory. This does not demonstrate either that there is no point in seeking some general descriptive account of education or that none will be forthcoming. In fact, it seems plain and utterly unsurprising that the natural context of education is one in which we take seriously the advancement of knowledge and understanding, see it as important to eliminate ignorance and error, prefer truth to falsity, aspire to rationality rather than irrationality and take seriously the idea of justifying our opinions and sentiments. The reason we are inspired by such ideals is that through the attainment of knowledge and understanding we come to make a better sense of the huge variety of different (kinds of) problems that confront us on a daily basis as we live our lives. As has many times been emphasized by many previous writers, education is a *cognitive enterprise*. Education is nothing if not about equipping individual minds with those ways of making sense of the world, physical, social and cultural, that at any given time in respect of any given culture are deemed to represent the best such ways as are available. This sense of education as an cognitive enterprise is nicely captured by the thought that education addresses 'the things of the mind' where the mind is that *active* agency through which we approach the world and through the exercise of which we come to terms with it. There is no need at this stage to commit ourselves to a wholesale belief that all those areas of human concern – morality, religion, aesthetics (say) – that so exercise us must have as their final object the revelation of moral, religious, aesthetic *truths*. But as an essentially cognitive enterprise, education can aid in the appreciation of that significance and those forms of reasoning so distinctive of them. In short, education can afford individuals access to the huge variety of ways in which human beings have over time made (a kind of) sense of their experience. It is within these contexts that we talk of social, moral, emotional, aesthetic and other kinds of development. It is in extending individual development in these areas that notions like truth, rationality and associated *epistemic* ideas find a natural home.

It would be a useful exercise to go back to the earlier list in this chapter of the different kinds of education we mark off, e.g. moral education, science education, maths education, etc., and see whether the above very general characterization of education as an enterprise carries conviction. It seems that it does. What the emphasis upon education does in all instances is highlight the ambition to 'initiate' individuals into these highly distinctive ways of making a sense of the concerns of the given subject matters. Thus the hoped for outcome of moral education is, at least, individuals who take moral matters seriously and understand why they are to be taken seriously along with the ability to handle, and make some sense of, moral issues. Making some sense of moral matters involves knowing the kinds of reasoning (and other) moves that allow for participation in moral debate, and even the achievement of some resolution. Whether the resolution of moral issues captures moral truths or lays bare moral facts is a deep issue. Though it is, I think, characteristic of moral debate that we conduct that debate as though there are moral truths to be grasped.

What is true of moral education is true of every other candidate on that list. The outcome of a successful education in one or other of those areas is the ability to conduct oneself in a manner such that confronted by a certain kind of problem an individual knows their way around. They can make sense of a certain kind of problem and move towards some kind of solution. Without that education he or she would be incapable of finding a way forward – certainly not, anyway, from within their own resources. Through coming to know appropriate things and coming to an appropriate understanding, sense can be made of the relevant dimensions of our human experience. Enhanced knowledge and understanding are the necessary preconditions of the human capacities of flexibility and adaptability, so fundamental to the achieving of desired human ends.

If the point being made needs further rehearsing reflect on the fact that someone deemed ineducable is someone who wholly lacks the capacity to come to know and understand, make any real sense of, the circumstances that will confront them. Someone who says that they found some set of circumstances 'a bit of an education' is an individual who as a consequence of that set of circumstances now sees things differently, has another kind of, or a deeper, understanding of whatever it might be than that possessed previously. We talk of the education of the emotions because through giving individuals another apprehension of the facts, getting them to see things differently, a person can be brought to the recognition that a certain emotional response is inappropriate or unwarranted. Through seeing events more truthfully, an individual might be able to understand more accurately the nature of their emotional response. My anger at my wife's (imagined) adultery can be transformed into pride when I come to know that all those Wednesday mornings with another man were not carnal occasions but rather occasions in which she quietly (and without letting on to me) went about the business of caring for the terminally ill. Someone who is self educated (as we say) is someone who persistently, systematically and purposively, sought the kind of knowledge and understanding that through the institutions of education we seek to deliver to all the members of our communities. It is possible to go on and on illustrating the general point: it is only against the background of *epistemic* notions like knowledge and understanding, truth and falsity, rationality and irrationality, making sense of, that talk of education enjoys currency. Without such a context, talk of education would lack significance, be an instance of 'language idling'.

It is important to recognize the extremely general nature of this claim. In talking of education as geared to the promotion of truth, knowledge and understanding, the enlargement of rationality, the making sense of the world in all its manifestations, we are not committing ourselves to any particular claims about the nature of truth. We live in an age that is assailing certain claims about what is involved for something to be known to be true, at least in so far as it is thought that notions like truth, rationality, knowledge and understanding commit us to an idea that there is a world out there that we can come to 'know' in some way that represents just 'how the world is'. The world is in a certain way quite separate from us and in no way dependent on our interests and purposes for how it actually is. Truth, rationality, objectivity, what is known, what is adequately understood, all offer us a guarantee that to the extent we have achieved them, we have captured an objective reality. On the contrary, it is argued, they simply reflect ways in which we humans have come to interpret and make a certain sense of things. In some deep sense, these notions to which we attach such significance are conventional rather than revelatory of 'how things really are'. The immediately foregoing is the merest indication of the nature of the debate swirling around in certain circles. However, for our purposes it is not necessary to engage in the debate. The claim that is being made in respect of the concept of education is that significant talk about education can only take place in a context that utilizes (whatever the final status of such notions) talk of knowledge, truth, error, falsity, understanding and the like. It is to say that any society possessed of these ideas can intelligibly embrace the idea of education. What is left entirely open is what the substance will be of any programmes devoted to the education of a people. It is entirely feasible that from the outside we can comfortably talk of education going on within a society and culture that is not ours even if what is on offer in the name of education is something which would not (perhaps, could not) figure in any educational programme of ours.

In the name of what is viewed as the truth, in the name of what are seen as key to making sense of a social world, all kinds of topics and subject matters can be utilized in pursuit of education. What topics, what subject matters and how they are delivered are very much influenced by the aims and purposes of any educational programme.

Aims – At Last

It is a defining feature of humans that we act upon the world. We enjoy the capability of shaping events in the light of our beliefs as to how things are. Sometimes things do just happen to us, occasionally we have no control over our behaviour. However, the less control over our behaviour, the less we think of that behaviour as ours since it does not flow from or express our beliefs, hopes, fears, ambitions, purposes and the like. The presumption informing human behaviour is that there is a reason why someone did what he or she did. We expect some appropriate response to the question 'Why did you do that?' An appropriate response is a reason informing our action. Education over time refines our reason-giving capacities, enlarges those areas of our life over which the writ of reason-giving runs. All of this goes hand in hand with a deep belief that we have that education gives individuals a greater measure of control over their own lives. To the extent that individuals are denied, as we see it, the ability to exercise that control, we condemn whatever limits the human potential to be in charge of their lives. Thus it is that indoctrination attracts such a bad press in our liberal society. But I might already be going beyond more general talk of education and beginning to talk of a certain version of *liberal* education that we expect to see honoured in our own society. I do not want to be seen denying that societies not committed to liberal sentiments and principles can give their members something that is unproblematically to be viewed as a kind of education. It seems clear to me that introducing people to the ways in which in a given society things and events are made sense of is already to have gone a long way to encouraging the reason-giving capacity and hence educating people.

Educating individuals is a human activity. Necessarily it is subject to the questions 'Why are you doing this?', 'What are you striving to achieve?' No doubt over time educational practice might become unreflective, no doubt there will be times (like now in contemporary Britain) in which the asking of such questions about education, its aims and purposes, is discouraged or hijacked. But as a systematic human activity, aims will be being pursued. And on bringing to the surface those aims we might seek to persuade others to embrace other and, as we see it, better aims. Consider a typical list of candidates as the primary aims of education: the promotion of autonomy, the encouragement of a multicultural society, the producing of good Christians, the preservation of our culture, the development of a democratic citizenry, the promotion of economic development, the production of good and responsible citizens, the securing of a skilled workforce, the forging of a morally educated society, the furtherance of God's will on earth, the creation of a society at ease with itself, the elimination of racism and sexism in our society. One could go on spelling out a whole host of highly general ambitions which might provide overriding considerations informing our educational provision.

We have to recognize that the world is not so harmoniously ordered that no hard choices between our ostensible aims is necessary. Realistically we should recognize choices will have to be made. The pursuit of some aim or aims will be to the detriment of others. For instance, the determination to produce good Christian gentlemen might well fall foul of a serious commitment to the promotion of autonomy with its rejection of any idea that we as educators should seek to shape and mould individual minds in any particular direction except for taking responsibility for our own decisions. Again the promotion of autonomy might well not be served by the ambition to produce a workforce with those skills necessary for the nation's economic wellbeing. One could imagine a society at ease with itself precisely being one that self-confidently proclaimed the superiority of its own culture as against others struggling for recognition in that society. And so on. Putting it rather more formally, the values finding expression in the articulation of educational aims may well be incommensurable and therefore often in tension with each other.

An aim while guiding and shaping educational activity should be deliverable. This is a relatively modest demand. There is enough evidence to suggest that education can encourage, for example, a (greater) measure of autonomy in human affairs for us to be comfortable with autonomy as a realistic educational aim. Whether it actually recommends itself as an aim to be pursued will turn on other considerations.

Our discussion has been at a fairly high level of abstraction. Almost everything so far said is compatible with all talk *about* education and its aims. When it comes to the actual and substantive discussion of which should be the main concern of education, the situation is radically transformed. All such discussion must be contextualized. Serious discussion about what the aims of education should be, or whether this or that set of aims should inform our educational practices, cannot be conducted in a vacuum. We have to talk (for instance) about real governments or other agencies located in this or that economic, cultural, moral, political context(s) looking to education to bring about desirable changes at both the individual and social level through those institutions charged with delivering education. We have to talk about individuals spelling out their best hopes for education against the background of a whole welter of beliefs of different kind which inform and shape their educational ambitions. The aims that are laid down are, to a very important degree, an expression of a whole outlook on the world – aims are not easily separable from ideological stances. Education has the capacity to change (transform, even) individuals in important ways, it has the capacity to realize the potential of people in all kinds of ways and along a whole range of dimensions. Denying people education stunts their development, denying them education prevents them flourishing in ways they might otherwise flourish. Human beings are born with all kinds of talents, dispositions, propensities, inclinations. Education can, in a benign way, aid in the development of those potentialities. But we have to recognize that as humans we cannot do everything, achieve in everything, enjoy all the satisfactions living can deliver. We must expect that those who look to education to enhance both individual and social life will have deep down some preferred vision of how things can be for humans. Characteristically our best hopes for individuals are importantly touched by our best hopes for how our social life can be. The history of political theory abounds with schemes of thought giving expression to a sense of mankind and its possibilities. It is not to the point here to explore the logic of those different visions; suffice it to say that as theorists operate with different pictures of human nature so we should expect their theories will portray for us different scenarios as to the ideal society.

It is often said that all education is political. Certainly one thing that seems clear is that educational theories of the kind associated with the great educational thinkers mentioned earlier – elaborate and well articulated accounts of the excellences to be produced grounded in, and justified by, a mix of empirical and normative propositions about human beings, human life and the world buttressed further by a series of statements about basic ends, moral principles of an ultimate kind, and so on – are very much the mirror image of an underlying political philosophy. Thus Plato's recommendations in *The Republic* are of a piece with his general social philosophy, Rousseau's *Emile* is consistent with his political theorizing and Dewey's educational theorizing is highly consonant with his overall philosophy. The relationship between underlying philosophical stances and educational theorising is not always so quite straightforward but educational recommendations are always grounded in deep sentiments and principles informing a theorist's outlook. The precise way in which ultimate commitments about the nature of the child, the kind of societies desired, whether humankind is aggressively selfish or capable of altruism, etc. find expression in educational theories, varies from instance to instance but pursued far enough it is possible to discern the coherence of educational recommendations – both as to curriculum content and pedagogic practices – with such ultimate considerations.

It is often said that educational aims 'determine' curriculum content and pedagogical method. 'Determine' seems altogether too strong a word. It must be expected aims will *shape* curriculum content and pedagogy. After all what would it be to espouse certain aims and then provide teaching and learning that subverted the very possibility of achieving those aims? But it seems quite clear (and this is as true in education as anywhere else), that, as the adage has it, 'there is more than one way of skinning a cat'. The same aims are achievable via quite different approaches to learning and the determination of curriculum content. It is up to learning theorists to cast light on how it might be possible to deliver specified aims. It is an empirical matter which kinds of teaching and learning deliver or best promote certain key aims of education. Providing there is an intelligible connection between aims pursued and the means used, the 'how' of practice is an empirical matter.

Perhaps a little late in the day we should remind ourselves that in ordinary parlance, aims can be very general, more specific, lofty, lowly, long term, short term, overriding, dependent and so on. What they all have in common is that they provide goals to be achieved, something to measure success by. Our talk of aims has been about those aims that provide some overriding rationale for the entirety of our educational practice. What is done in the name of education is done because we have the aim or aims we do. Paulo Freire once said words to the effect that any action undertaken in the classroom for educational purposes embodies within itself an entire philosophy of education. If asked of any action while teaching 'Why did you do that?' a reason will be provided. As one asks at every further stage the question 'Why?' there is inevitably the elaboration of all that underlies the initial action. The end product is some large statement outlining the ultimate ambition(s) – aim(s) – informing the educational programme. No doubt, there is a lot more to be said about such a claim but it does nicely emphasize the importance of aims (in our sense) in providing some ultimate unifying theme for our educational activities.

Liberal Education: A Perspective On Aims

Given the need to contextualize talk of the ultimate or primary aims of education, what might be said about the main aims of education in our society? We purport to be a liberal, pluralistic, democratic society. But spelling out the commitments that would characterize any society aspiring to those labels is a major task of political philosophers. Impressionistically such a society would lay emphasis upon the primacy and worth of the individual – individuals have rights and entitlements that should be respected, they have correlative responsibilities that demand the recognition of the claims of other individuals upon us. We are attached to the idea that individuals should enjoy responsibility for their own lives. This goes along with the belief typical of a main strand of liberal theory that the state should remain neutral as to the competing possibilities of the good life on offer within a diverse society like ours. It is no part of the state's job to promote a distinctive lifestyle, or ideology for general acceptance. Individuals should be allowed to order and shape their own lives. It is allowing individuals to do so which, more than anything else, gives expression to our respect for their dignity.

It can easily be seen that the proclaiming of the promotion of autonomy as the primary educational goal is very much of a piece with underlying liberal philosophy. The role of education – rooted as it is in, and inspired by, the commitment to knowledge and understanding – in delivering autonomy is plain. The successful pursuit of knowledge and understanding equips individuals with the wherewithal to make a better sense of their lives. In freeing them of ignorance, in encouraging the use of critical rationality premised upon the desire to understand more accurately what is going on and happening both to them and in the world, individuals will move towards autonomy. Whatever autonomy is, it certainly embraces the idea of self-determining individuals making decisions that are their own. In achieving autonomy, freedom in human affairs is advanced. The enlargement of knowledge and understanding promotes the creation of autonomous persons. That very knowledge and understanding further encourages the possibility of the fulfilment of many of the goals that people look to education to promote, e.g. the governmental desire for a skilled workforce. There is no reason to suppose that the encouragement of autonomy is at variance with such an ambition. It is significantly more doubtful whether an overriding concern with producing a skilled workforce through our educational system is as likely to produce autonomous individuals. As a general aim, autonomy is a peculiarly liberal ambition which in no way detracts from the importance to be attached to the need for a flourishing economy. How individuals exercise their autonomy is never going to be quite predictable. There is no reason to suppose, however, that the exercise of autonomy is detrimental to much that we believe to be socially desirable. All that said, we have to live with the possibility that the exercise of autonomy in human affairs will often be uncomfortable and not conforming to our prejudices. But it is precisely the challenging of our prejudices and received ways of thinking and doing things that is autonomy's greatest contribution to our affairs and concerns.

So the argument might run. I have suggested that any overriding aim that specifies what education should be about, or try to accomplish, can be seen and understood only within the context of a whole set of commitments and beliefs that form a general stance on the social and political possibilities open to humans. I have sketched very briefly indeed the start of an argument that might seek to justify an insistence upon autonomy as the key educational aim. In the event of conflict (real and apparent) between people as to which candidates for educational aims should enjoy priority there has to be recourse to argument. If I am right, disagreement about ultimate educational ends is a species of moral and political debate. Parties to the debate will rehearse what seem to them to be the considerations that justify the emphasis upon one aim or set of aims as rightly enjoying supremacy. It is a matter of trying to persuade another to come to share your distinctive vision of what is best for individuals and the wider society. Whether we consider that such debate can be resolved will depend on our judgement about the rationality or otherwise of such political or moral debate. Certainly parties operating within the same ideological framework might well be able to come to an intellectual accommodation in the event of some agreement as to the facts and having eliminated conceptual confusions. The crucial issue is whether competing ideologues discussing educational aims can achieve a meeting of minds such that argument can be carried forward. We certainly behave as if these deep questions are susceptible to reasoned debate. In the end we might have to live with the thought that we are compelled to keep the dialogue going

Response to 'The Aims of Education'

Ian Davies

In Chapter 1 you have read about the aims of education. Or, perhaps we should say that you have read Ian Gregory's views about the aims of education. There is a difference between these two statements. While Ian Gregory is a philosopher and an expert on education, he ultimately gives us his opinion. We respect his opinion. His judgements have been formed after many years of serious and rigorous thought. But, it remains an opinion and it is important for us now to consider the nature of his argument. Following what was said in the introduction to the book, it will not surprise the reader that I am about to raise some significant reservations about his arguments.

It is, however, first necessary to clarify the nature of those arguments. Unless I do this, even if only briefly, it will be hard to go beyond a sense that Ian Gregory has merely presented us with the obvious truth or plain common sense. In essence he makes five arguments:

- Education is 'a good thing'.
- We can agree on how education should be characterized. It has a unified and coherent purpose.
- Education is largely a cognitive matter in which people's capacity to think rationally is developed.
- Education allows us to pursue the truth and we should resist

attempts to persuade of the wisdom of adopting what can be called, very generally, a post-modernist approach.

- The principal purpose of education is to develop people's capacity to become autonomous.

I will take each of the above arguments in turn and suggest that we should be rather more cautious.

Education Is 'A Good Thing'

This is an attractive argument. Those engaged in education as teachers, students or in any other role wish to believe that they are somehow on the side of the angels. I am in the process of devoting my professional life to education and am rather reluctant to consider any suggestion that I might be wasting my time! A modern society needs an education system. Of course, we cannot rely on some naïve primitivist ideal in which we go back to nature. Rousseau may have proclaimed the value of a natural education in the eighteenth century but I would not suggest that we become castaways from reality. I agree with Ian Gregory in so far as education *may* be a good thing. And yet, we should not be so complacent. Rather, I wish to draw attention to the real meaning of the views expressed in Chapter 1.

When Ian Gregory uses the word 'education' he often makes little or no distinction between that and 'schooling'. We can see that he has written that 'education . . . is something that is systematically and purposively pursued'. He feels that where schools are not established 'we wish it could be otherwise'. What he seems to mean is that we should believe that the establishment of schools is a good thing. Now this is very controversial. Although we are bombarded on a daily basis by representatives of massive international bureaucracies that insist that we should have ever more schooling, we suggest that it is important not to be carried along too swiftly by this swelling tide of self-congratulation. A few years ago writers such as Reimer and Illich were proclaiming a very different vision. Reimer (1971) claimed that 'school is dead'. Illich (1973) suggested that the future lay not in more schooling but in 'deschooling'. Learning webs based on small groups would be the answer rather than ever more schooling. Althusser (1972a) writing from a neo-Marxist perspective saw society as dominated by a range of repressive state apparatuses (RSAs) such as the army and police, and ideological state apparatuses (ISAs) such as schools. Even authors who were seen as less ideologically biased came up with equally radical critiques. Dore (1997), for example, claimed that we were (in the 1970s!) suffering from the diploma disease in which ever more qualifications were required by candidates applying for employment. In the twenty-first century, we see an expansion in the number of undergraduates (currently about one-third of all 18-year-olds instead of the figure of approximately 10 per cent in 1980) and the increasing length of undergraduate courses (many science degrees now last for four instead of three years).

Do we really have that much additional knowledge that must be learnt? Or, more importantly, do we see that schools have been so effective in developing a more knowledgeable society and reducing the problems that we face? The straightforward and honest answer is that we have a continuing scramble for the scarce goods that we value. Educational qualifications are one way in which a society can make it appear as if scarce goods (such as higher incomes and status) are being allocated fairly. Of course, authors mentioned above, such as Illich and Reimer, are now deeply unfashionable. But we need to realize that education cannot exist in some sort of pure form. Education is, as Freire (1990) argued, always *for* something. Teachers, according to Freire, are either for liberation or for oppression. Or, to use a slightly different perspective, in a debate about economics, education could either be seen as a way in which the state invests in its own future or the way that it allows students and others to consume. We really need to see what purpose Ian Gregory has decided it should have before we accept his arguments that his form of education is a good thing. This is a question that will be pursued in the remaining part of this response. The simple proposition, however, that education is in itself, and especially in the way that it has been characterized by Ian Gregory, always a good thing, can easily be rejected.

Education Has a Unified and Coherent Purpose

Much of what was said in the above section shows that education does not have a unified purpose. It should be recognized that some may not wish to accept my ideas as they relate too strongly to the work of authors such as Illich and Althusser who were at their most influential over 30 years ago. However, the arguments outlined above do have contemporary relevance. It is necessary only to see current debates about how schools can demonstrate achievement. Schools are judged on their capacity to achieve good examination pass rates. Seventy per cent of pupils achieving 5 GCSEs (examinations normally taken at age 16) at grades A, B or C is the ticket to sublime respectability. Invitations to the government department for education (currently named the Department for Education and Skills) to explain one's success, more money for individuals in the form of performance-related pay, and favourable comment in the local and national press all await these high achievers. Of course, some schools will forever find it difficult to achieve in this way. A variety of factors, including the predominant social class within the school student body and the proportion of pupils who have English as a first language, mean that some schools will want to emphasize other forms of achievement. Some will emphasize the pastoral care system, or the range of community activities, or the opportunities for sport or the arts. In fact the government knows that it too must recognize these different emphases and achievements. If it does not, then the schools that have been told to operate in the market will either go out of business or will continue to receive pupils for the purpose only of branding them as failures. The recent introduction of specialist schools recognizes this reality. Without diverse targets the education system would collapse immediately into a two-tier framework of winners and losers. A single scale for achievement obviously and simply means that almost half of the school population is to be regarded as below average. The attempt to provide a number of ways to achieve will, of course, eventually be seen as something of a smokescreen which allows those from more prosperous areas to succeed in the areas that really matter (like GCSE pass grades) but this will take some time to be noticed. For the moment the hope of schools to achieve success in a specialist but low status area will disguise the true purpose of diversity. This is recognized when, despite his other comments, Ian Gregory knows that education seems normally to be 'discouraged or hijacked'. The reasons for this sort of diversity may provide, rather perversely, a sort of coherence but it does not seem one that is worth having.

Finally, there may be a more positive way of arguing against Ian Gregory's position. He himself recognizes the significance of diversity when he emphasizes the need for autonomy. The variety of theories about education, he suggests 'will portray for us different scenarios as to the ideal society'. Whatever he may say about the systematic and purposive nature of education he does not really seem to believe that it exists. So, either because of the rather negative political purposes that require a negative diversity, or due to Ian Gregory's own idealistic and more positive liberal reasons, his position that education is coherent and unified cannot be justified.

Education is Largely a Cognitive Matter in which People's Capacity to Think Rationally is Developed

Ian Gregory and others assert that 'education is a cognitive enterprise'. This, to continue the discussion from the previous section, is said to be what gives education its supposed coherence. I too believe that cognitive matters are vitally important but I do not agree that everything that happens in the name of education is cognitive. Indeed, as I have already rejected Ian Gregory's claim that we should not see education as being a unified enterprise, it should be now relatively straightforward to deal with the specific area that he suggests provides that supposed unity. Simply, although the cognitive is important it is not everything. It is somewhat surprising that Ian Gregory supplies a long list of 'educations' (moral education, science education, maths education, etc.) only to represent them all as being fundamentally cognitive. Perhaps he really means that those areas that are not cognitive do not really matter as much as others?

We should initially and briefly explore a few positive points that could be made to support Ian Gregory's position. He could be arguing for a very subtle expression of the necessary interplay between the intellect, the emotions, values and practical skills. Perhaps what he means by 'cognitive' is actually a complex interaction between all these areas? Also he is, possibly, developing his arguments in the light of some of the criticisms that have been made of Howard Gardner's ideas (e.g. White, 1998). There may be problems if one believes, as Gardner does, that multiple intelligences allow for significant and fundamental variation between patterns of thinking.

And yet, Ian Gregory's continuing search for some sort of coherence should not lead us astray. All learning should not be subsumed under the title of the cognitive. An important part of the educational process, of course, is to allow learners to develop, or simply to have the opportunity to express, a sense of wonder. We may want at certain points for learners to understand in a cognitive manner the intricacies of a piece of music by Bach or Beethoven. Musicians and musicologists need to undertake work that has a clear conceptual base and which relies on cognitive mastery. However, there is also an educational function in simply listening to music, watching dance, singing, playing in a way that is inspiring or simply fun. It would be most worrying if a school allowed artistic activities only in the pursuit of cognitive aims. Furthermore, education should provide learners with opportunities to have an impact. The precise nature of that impact is not a matter only for schools to consider. But I do agree with Ian Gregory that 'Making some sense of moral matters involves knowing the kinds of reasoning (and other) moves that allow for participation in moral debate, and even the achievement of some resolution'. In other words, skills that can be exercised in the 'real' world where resources are given to some and not others are a part of the educational process. The cognitive plays a significant and vitally important part in that process but there are aspects of this debate that mean that learners rely on far more than the cognitive. Making one's voice heard (literally and metaphorically) is not only a cognitive matter. Unless we are careful, restricting the scope of educational activity to the cognitive will lead some people to feel that the questions that educationalists deal with are 'academic'. It is worrying that when we say that something is merely 'academic' we normally mean that it simply does not matter. This is to be resisted.

Education allows us to Pursue the Truth and we should Resist Attempts to Persuade us of the Wisdom of Adopting what can be called, very generally, a Post-modernist Approach

I would not want to disagree too sharply with the general thrust of Ian Gregory's argument as shown in the above heading. Post-modernism is already an outdated and largely disregarded way of thinking about the world (e.g. see Marwick, 2001). Perhaps it is necessary briefly to look at the meaning of this word. Jenkins (1995), presenting himself as a post-modernist, has explained that:

> Today we live within the general condition of postmodernity. We do not have a choice about this. For postmodernity is not an ideology or a position we can choose to subscribe to or not; postmodernity is precisely our condition: it is our fate. And this condition has been caused by the general failure . . . of the attempt, from around the 18th century in Europe, to bring about through the application of reason, science and tech-nology, a level of personal and social wellbeing within social formations which, legislating for an increasingly generous eman-cipation of their citizens/subjects, we might characterise by saying that they were trying, at best, to become 'human rights communities'. (p. 6)

Such gloomy thoughts need to be rejected. They are both illogical (the overarching view of the post-modernists seems to be that an overarching view is not possible) and elitist (if we cannot approach the truth then the history and condition of 'minority' groups is less likely to be recognized by those who are more powerful). Detailed and generally convincing demolition jobs have been done on post-modernism (e.g. Appleby, Hunt and Jacob, 1994; Evans, 1997) and need not be added to here.

And yet, there is something rather too simple and straightforward about the way in which Ian Gregory encourages us to embrace 'the truth'. This is probably the most difficult of questions and it is dealt with by him very briefly. It would be unfair to make too much of the relative lack of consideration of this matter in such a short chapter and yet it does seem to be a fundamental part of his approach to thinking about education. We really do need to know more about the nature of the truth that is proposed and the ways that are suggested for approaching it. It seems that the truth that is proposed actually relates to a way of knowing for a particular purpose. While he does not suggest it is the job of teachers to establish specific beliefs in learners, it is, he seems to suggest, their task to promote a highly politicized form of viewing the world. While this view is somewhat hidden under the innocuous title of 'autonomy', the nature of what he is suggesting needs further analysis in the next and final section of this response.

The Principal Purpose of Education is to Develop People's Capacity to become Autonomous

It is in the search for autonomy that Ian Gregory's liberal ideals become most apparent. Much of what is discussed above is given clearer meaning in the light of the emphasis upon autonomy. It is not, he argues, for the state 'to promote a distinctive life style . . . Individuals should be allowed to order and shape their own lives'. Neither is it for the philosophy of education as a discipline to steer us in the right direction. 'Its ambitions', according to Ian Gregory, 'are *clarificatory* rather than driven by the desire to get us to act in ways recommended and inspired by any educational theorist's "phil-osophy of education"'. This is attractive as it makes a distinction between the state and academic disciplines on the one hand and, on the other, the individuals who take action in the name of a better society. Whereas we can hope that too much power will not be claimed by the former, we can encourage individuals to use their autonomy to act positively or to be checked by others who are also acting autonomously.

However, this is, of course, very ideologically biased and open to challenge. We are wondering what precisely is the distinction between Ian Gregory's approach and that, for example, of James

Tooley (2000, p. iv) who wants to make 'a case for reclaiming education from the state'. These autonomous individuals who would be part of this new education system are not as strongly a part of the civic republican tradition in which a greater sense of responsibility is emphasized. There are three questions that need to be addressed if such an emphasis is placed on the value of liberalism:

- What, if anything, provides the 'glue' to hold society together?
- What limits to unacceptable action are imposed?
- When failure occurs in our ambitions to develop a better society who will be held to account?

The answers to these questions are not given in Ian Gregory's piece. In practice such an emphasis on a liberal approach would seem to rely too heavily on superficial notions such as the (in)famous comment by Thatcher that there is no such thing as society. It actively encourages us to 'bowl alone' rather than to work and socialize with others (Putnam, 1999). It relies on the primacy of individual wealth generation and the effective exclusion of less privileged groups who by their very poverty and their adherence to a devalued culture reveal their individual failure. All pluralist societies must deal with very complex problems associated with the existence of the spectrum of beliefs and practices. The question is not whether there should be such a spectrum but rather how wide it should be and who should decide how the polar ends of that spectrum are characterized (Dahl, 1982). The post-modern approach (not post-modernism itself) allows for some very fundamental questions to be asked. We need to ask which groups are receiving more scarce goods than others and whether this reflects a just society? These are questions that have educational purposes. They are not necessarily to be pursued within a society that sees itself only in terms of isolated individuals. The attraction of the liberal approach is that it allows us to think we have individual autonomy to ask those questions and to make things better. The reality is that self-interest becomes a more powerful factor in the determination of educational policies than the consideration of group as well as individual needs and the pursuit of justice.

Activities

The following questions are designed to encourage further reflection upon key issues raised in Chapter 1. There are no easy answers to these questions, they demand serious and sustained thought. They are among the most fundamental questions we can raise about education, its aims and purposes and how it might be delivered.

Key Questions

What might be meant by saying 'education is essentially a cognitive enterprise'? Reflect on the implications – if any – of your answer for how we set about teaching what we teach in the name of education.

Make out a case for a common curriculum. What subjects, and why, should be part of any common curriculum you favour?

To what extent do you think Ian Davies is correct in saying that: 'simply listening to music, watching dance, singing, playing in a way that is inspiring or simply fun' can be proper educative activities? And if they are, is this incompatible with the notion that education is an essentially cognitive enterprise? Justify your belief.

How far do you think Ian Gregory is committed to the idea that schooling is a good thing because he believes education is 'a good thing'?

What functions do schools serve? Are their non-educational functions more or less important than any educational functions they serve?

'Better schools, not deschooling should be the way forward.' Do you agree or not? Spell out the reasons for your opinion.

What aim or aims do you think most important in education and why? What weight do you attach to autonomy as an educational aim?

Suggestions for Reading

Barrow, Robin and Woods, Ron (1975) (3rd Edn) *An Introduction to the Philosophy of Education*. London: Methuen. A lively challenging introduction to key topics in the philosophy of education.

Hirst, Paul H. (1974) *Knowledge and the Curriculum*. London: RKP. A series of influential papers on curricular content issues. Includes his key text 'Liberal Education and the Nature of Knowledge'. Still bears reading, well worth taking the effort to understand.

Kleinig, John (1982) *Philosophical Issues in Education*. London: Croom Helm. A radical but sophisticated philosophical take on topics in the philosophy of education. Illuminating discussion of Illich and deschooling. A good critique of liberal philosophy of education.

O'Hear, Anthony (1981) *Education, Society and Human Nature*. London: RKP. Covers key issues in a challenging and philosophically informed manner. Well worth reading.

Peter, R. S. (1966) *Ethics and Education*. London: George Allen & Unwin. Seminal text in the contemporary burgeoning of 'The Philosophy of Education'. Contains his very influential analysis of education and its aims. Further elaboration of these initial thoughts can be found in his text (with Paul Hirst): *The Logic of Education*. London: RKP (1970).

Wringe, Colin (1988) *Understanding Educational Aims*. London: Unwin Hyman. A clear comprehensive survey of possible aims of education ranging from the promotion of autonomy through causes of racial and sexual justice to making young people productive workers. A strong plea for the centrality of the cognitive in education.

Suggested Practical Activities

1. Draw up a list of familiar clichés surrounding education, e.g. education is of the whole person, etc. Do they have enough in common to allow us to say anything of any value of a *general*

nature about education? If not, what does that tell us about Education with a big 'E'?

2. Get six individuals to draw a list of six aims they look to education to promote. Analyse their lists, see what they have in common, how they differ. Is it possible to find a way of reconciling their differences? If it is, how do you do it? If not, why not and what are the implications of such a failure?

3. Taking as your inspiration one of the great educational theorists try and spell out in a systematic manner what your 'educational philosophy' is. Do it within 500 words listing your key aim or aims, and how they (it) fit(s) into your general ideological outlook.

4. Devise for a class of 14-year-olds a timetable for the week. You have unlimited resources. The only constraint upon you is that the school day runs from 9.00am to 4.00pm. How did you set about the task and what kinds of considerations influenced your curricular choices and the time you gave to them?

5. As for Suggestion 4 but get two friends to do the same. Sit down and discuss the issues thrown up by comparing your timetables.

6. Write a critique of your own schooling. Did you receive a good education? How might it have been better? Did it advance your autonomy and if so, how? Did it equip you for the world of work?

A Note to the Reader about Chapters 2 and 3 from Nick McGuinn

Chapters 2 and 3 engage with educational ideas from the perspective of literature. Two texts in particular are used as a starting-point for the exploration of key concepts and issues: Peter Dickinson's novel *A Bone from a Dry Sea*, published in 1992, and William Shakespeare's play *The Tempest*, written and performed around 1611/1612 (Kermode, 1964). I want to stress the phrase 'starting-point' here. You do not have to be a literature student or an authority on Shakespeare and his language to follow the arguments under discussion. Background information about the texts is supplied within the chapters as appropriate. This is particularly true in the case of *The Tempest*, where I have tried to anticipate any potential confusion which my use of quotations from the play might cause by adding a brief explanation of what is happening in my accompanying commentary. It is more important that you understand the gist of what is being said than that you worry about who 'Sycorax' might be or what 'scammels' are. Having said that, I would be delighted to know that reading these two chapters had inspired you to study these or other of the 'starting-point' texts in their entirety. They are all well worth the effort!

CHAPTER 2

How and Why Do We Learn?

Nick McGuinn

In 1992, the author Peter Dickinson published a novel called *A Bone from a Dry Sea*. Dickinson is well known for his ability to present young people with challenging intellectual material in fictional form. This book is no exception. Part of the story is set in the Africa of four million years ago and concerns a young hominid called Li.

The novel poses an interesting question. What was it, Dickinson wonders, that enabled our earliest ancestors to make the momentous conceptual breakthrough which has brought *homo sapiens*, uniquely, to the state of development we know today? Looking through the eyes of Li, he tries to imagine a key moment of transition. The passage is worth quoting at length:

> From the shade of the tree, Li studied the plain. She felt excited but tense. She had never been so far from the tribe alone. She didn't know what there was to be afraid of – there could be no sharks out here and she'd never seen a leopard, but the instinct was still there, deep inside. Another instinct made her climb into the crotch of the tree, and on up until she was well above ground level. Now she relaxed a little.
>
> The tree had been flat-topped once, but an earthquake had tilted it so that on one side its branches touched the ground and on the other they lifted enough for her to see out beneath them. She stared, amazed, at the distance. Before her lay the

marsh. From the shore it had seemed endless, but now beyond it she saw a wavering line of blue, rising to peaks from two of which thin trails of smoke drifted skyward. She recognized them because there was another such peak at the centre of the island. Sometimes it flamed, sometimes it rumbled or groaned, but mostly it merely smoked, peaceful and harmless.

Li stared entranced at the view. The fifty miles or so of island shore which was the tribe's territory was all she had ever known, all the world there was. Now, over there beyond the marshes, she saw another world, immense.

Cramp broke the trance, making her shift her position. Then a flick of movement caught her eye, speed followed by stillness, like a minnow in a pool. It had happened where the spread twigs of the tree swept down to the earth. Inquisitive, she climbed down and crept across to see.

The spider was crouched over its prey, bouncing gently on its springy legs. Spiders were no good to eat. The bug it had caught might have been but Li wasn't hungry. She wanted to see what the spider would do. She crouched and watched while the spider dragged the bug clear of the insect-size track along which it had been scuttling. It climbed into the twigs above the track and rapidly wove a coarse, loose web, then returned to earth and stretched a couple of threads across the path. It moved into the shadows and waited. So did Li.

Nothing happened. Her absorption dwindled. She became aware of the dry, alien plain around her, and her distance from the tribe. Every insect-click, every faint rustle, might be a danger-sound. She must go back. But first she needed to know what the spider was up to. There was no reason for the need, no purpose or use in knowing. It was the mere knowledge that mattered.

Moving as carefully as if she'd been stalking a minnow she pulled a grass stem from a tussock and, starting some distance from the web, trailed the seed-head along the path. It moved jerkily, like a crawling bug. As it touched the threads the web tumbled from above, tangling loosely round it, and the spider had leaped and was crouching over it to inspect its prey. Li couldn't see what had triggered the web to fall.

She watched the spider strip the remains of web from the seed-head and eat them. The stem was too heavy for it to draw the seed-head clear of the path, so it chose a new place, built another web-trap and waited. Li peered closely, trying to see how the web was made, but it was too complicated for her. The sense of danger returned, overwhelming her longing for knowledge, so she gave up and returned to the beach.

Li rejoins her tribe where they are dozing in the sun on a nearby beach; but she cannot rest:

> the excitement of thought kept her awake. There were two pictures in her mind – the minnows in the pool and the web dropping from the twigs. Northward there were rock-pools with minnows in them. A yellow one was especially delicious, but almost impossible to catch. But if she could make a web . . . How . . . ? With what . . . ?
>
> Towards evening, she crossed the dunes again and collected the longest stems she could find. Returning to the beach she scooped away the burning surface, making a cooler hollow where she could sit and work at the problem, stopping only when it was too dark to see. She got nowhere. The stems were brittle and wouldn't stay together, her fingers didn't understand what she wanted them to do, but she remained, absorbed. The failures themselves were knowledge, feeding her need.

Li cannot let the problem go:

> In the night the notion had come to her that they [the grass stems with which she had originally tried to make her web] were brittle because they were dry, and if she wetted them she might have more luck. This helped a little, but soon the sun became too hot for further work on shore, and in the water the grass stems floated about uncontrollably, so she gave up.
>
> Then she remembered that she had sometimes seen bigger pieces of gourd-fibre, so she went and searched the dunes till she found one about as large as her spread hand. At the noon tide she tried it out. She was still thinking of minnows. She hadn't intended to use it to catch shrimps – she could do that with her hands – and only wanted to see how the mesh worked, but at her first trawl she found several transparent bodies wriggling on the net. Delicately she picked them out, calling *Come-and-see* to Ma-ma. (Dickinson, 1992, pp. 26–9)

Dickinson's account of the process by which Li learns how to make her shrimping-net raises some interesting questions about western society's attitudes towards teaching, learning and assessment. Consider first of all the setting in which this episode takes place. Li is on her own when she has her life-changing encounter with the spider. She has left the security of her tribe behind, daring to put her life at risk in order to see and learn new things. I do not think it is any coincidence that the act of learning takes place in a tree, nor that enlightenment is bestowed by a creature from a different species. If, in Dickinson's narrative, Li represents our 'first mother', then it is not surprising that we might make connections between her experience and that of Eve who, according to the Book of Genesis, was tempted by a serpent to taste of the Tree of Good and Evil:

> And the woman said unto the serpent, We may eat of the fruit of the trees of the garden:
> But of the fruit of the tree which is in the midst of the garden, God hath said, Ye shall not eat of it, neither shall ye touch it, lest ye die.
> And the serpent said unto the woman, Ye shall not surely die: For God doth know that in the day ye eat thereof, then your eyes shall be opened, and ye shall be as gods, knowing good and evil. (Gen. 3: 2–4)

This story from Genesis is perhaps the most potent example of a powerful metanarrative which lies embedded in western thought. Throughout our culture, we find stories which tell us that the desire to know, to step beyond the boundaries of the conventional and the familiar, is something about which we feel deeply ambivalent. For centuries, Christian ideology traced the ills of this world back to the temptation of Eve and in doing so made her a scapegoat for human suffering.

And yet, the individual who risks everything for the sake of knowledge can also be regarded as heroic. The Greek myth of Prometheus provides an example. Prometheus incurred the wrath of the gods by stealing fire from heaven because he felt compassion for human beings and wanted to do something to alleviate their misery. Echoes of the Prometheus myth – like the story of Eve – have resonated through our culture. For the nineteenth-century poet Shelley, Prometheus' quest for forbidden knowledge was unquestionably a good thing. Shelley described Prometheus as: 'the type of the highest perfection of moral and intellectual nature, impelled by the purest and the truest motives to the best and noblest ends' (Matthews, 1970, p. 205). After all, the gift of fire has contributed immeasurably to humanity's wellbeing and Prometheus put himself at risk, not for personal gain, but for the welfare of others. Shelley's wife, Mary, however, took a different view. Fire from heaven can be used to cook our food and warm our bodies – but it can also be put to evil and destructive purposes. Mary Shelley gave her famous novel *Frankenstein* the sub-title *The Modern Prometheus*. When the protagonist, Victor Frankenstein, strikes out alone to seek forbidden knowledge, he discovers the secret of life itself and uses that discovery to create a monster which turns against its creator and attempts to destroy him and the world he inhabits.

Viewed from this perspective, Li seems an unlikely Prometheus. True, she might be regarded as heroic in that she braves dangers and explores unfamiliar territory on her own in order to satisfy her quest for knowledge; but learning how to construct a humble shrimping-net is hardly to be equated with deliberate defiance of the gods or of sacred taboos. Nevertheless, Prometheus, Victor Frankenstein and Li are similar in that, for each of them, learning takes place within a moral context and has moral consequences. Once Prometheus has stolen fire from heaven, the gods cannot take it back. Once Victor Frankenstein has created his monster, he cannot uncreate him. Once Li has invented her shrimping-net, she cannot uninvent it. The important question is: What will she do with her knowledge?

Li has several options. Having trawled for shrimps a number of times, she could tire of her invention, return to the tribe and say nothing about it. To do this would be akin to withholding heavenly fire: it would deny the tribe access to a tool which might revolutionize their whole way of life for the better. Or, Li could choose to keep her knowledge to herself, setting up home under her tree and living off the plentiful supply of shrimps which her net would guarantee her. What could be more innocent than this? Had the sixteenth-century French philosopher Michel Montaigne observed her puzzling over the spider's web and searching for gourd fibres, he would have hailed Li as a perfect child of nature, untouched by civilisation. In the following extract from his essay *Of Cannibals* (reproduced here in John Florio's translation of 1603), Montaigne muses upon the true meaning of the word 'savage', contrasting what he perceives to be the purity of the recently discovered American 'Indians' with the corruption of their European colonizers:

> They [the Indians] are even savage, as we call those fruits wilde, which nature of her selfe . . . hath produced: whereas indeed . . . those which our selves have altered by our artificiall devices, and diverted from their common order, we should rather terme savage. In those are the true and most profitable

vertues, and naturall properties most lively and vigorous, which in these we have bastardized, applying them to the pleasures of our corrupted taste. And if notwithstanding, in divers fruits of those countries that were never tilled, we shall finde, that in respect of ours they are most excellent, and as delicate unto our taste; there is no reason, art should gaine the point of honour of our great and puissant mother Nature . . . (Quoted in Kermode, 1964, p. xxxv)

The picture is not as clear-cut, however, as Montaigne might like to think. As soon as Li trawls her shrimping-net through the pool, she ceases to be merely the recipient of nature's bounty and becomes instead one of Montaigne's real 'savages' – someone who diverts things of the natural world 'from their common order' and alters the environment by 'artificial devices'. Had Li not trawled that pool with her net, we would not today be living in a world where vast factory ships decimate the fish-stocks of the world by hoovering the sea-beds for their harvest. If Li takes this second option, keeps her discovery to herself and decides to live off the shrimps in her private pool, how long will it be until, no longer able to replenish their stocks faster than she can net them, the shrimps are wiped out? What happens then to Li – or to the other creatures who also relied upon the shrimps in that particular pool for their food? Do they die out too, or do they all go searching for another pool to destroy?

There is a third option for Li. I will explain what it is at the end of this chapter. Before doing that, however, I want to focus more closely on Li herself. What does her behaviour in this extract tell us about the ways in which human beings learn?

What was it about Li that she should be the one who discovered how to make the shrimping-net? To answer this question, we need to consider the contrasting influences of 'nature' and 'nurture'. We could argue that it was Li's nurture – her upbringing – which empowered her. As a child, Li will have experienced the process of 'learning by doing within the family' (Bowles, 1983, p. 28). Her tribe will have taught her the physical and mental skills she needs to survive. From them, for example, she will have learnt how to distinguish life-sustaining food sources, like shrimps, from life-threatening ones. She will have learnt how to tune all her senses so finely that she can actually flourish in what is a potentially hostile environment. They will have taught her those skills of foraging and observation without which she would not have been capable of noticing or studying the spider's actions in the first place. From the tribe, too,

Li will have acquired the belief-system by which she makes sense of her world. Dickinson explains in the novel that they spend their lives moving up and down the coast, following the migratory patterns of the shoals of shrimp, just as their ancestors have done for countless generations. This will have taught Li that tradition, stability and continuity are good and that the focus of her existence should be the beach and shallows of the shoreline. By the same token, change, innovation and the desire to turn away from the sea and explore the hinterland of the African continent are to be regarded as undesirable.

There is something about Li as a person, however, which causes her to defy the value-system of her tribe, just as Prometheus defies the gods or Victor Frankenstein defies the laws of nature. She regards the possibility of change as exciting rather than threatening. When she looks out from her tree, we are told that she 'stared, amazed, at the distance', that she was 'entranced at the view'. She understands that the huge African hinterland opening up before her might not be a place of unknown terror but 'another world, immense'. Christopher Columbus and Neil Armstrong would have understood how she felt. Li is also inquisitive: she likes to know why things are as they are. When the spider catches her eye, she creeps down to take a closer look, not in order to see whether it was good to eat or not (which would have been the conventional tribal response) but simply because she 'wanted to see what the spider would do'. This urge to know is so strong that it even overrides her deepest survival instincts:

> Every insect-click, every faint rustle, might be a danger-sound. She must go back. But first she needed to know what the spider was up to. There was no reason for the need, no purpose or use in knowing. It was the mere knowledge that mattered.

Finally, Li is capable, not only of responding to change, but actually of effecting change herself. Instead of simply waiting to see what the spider would do of its own accord, she decides to speed up the process of enquiry by devising an experiment:

> Moving as carefully as if she'd been stalking a minnow she pulled a grass stem from a tussock and, starting some distance from the web, trailed the seed-head along the path. It moved jerkily, like a crawling bug. As it touched the threads the web tumbled from above, tangling loosely round it, and the spider had leaped and was crouching over it to inspect its prey. Li couldn't see what had triggered the web to fall.

Dickinson portrays Li as someone very special. Like Prometheus and Victor Frankenstein again, she seems to be set apart from her peers, uniquely blessed (or perhaps cursed?) with the ability to unlock secrets and to make discoveries. The gift of insight is granted to her in moments of revelation, almost as if she were a shaman or visionary: 'In the night the notion had come to her that they [the grass stems with which she had originally tried to make her web] were brittle because they were dry, and if she wetted them she might have more luck.'

If we accept Dickinson's account of the way in which learning takes place here, we have to ask ourselves a number of questions. What would have happened if Li's sister, say, had been the one who sat in the tree and observed the spider? Would she have been equally capable of making the conceptual links between web and net? Or would she simply have dismissed the spider as inedible, lost interest, and gone back to the safety of the beach? And what would Li's brother have done? Would a male hominid have reacted differently from a female in this situation? Beaten its chest in defiance of the vast otherness of the African hinterland and then stamped on the spider in a show of strength, perhaps? In other words, is the logical conclusion to Dickinson's argument that only an elite few are capable of intellectual insight? If that is the case, why bother educating the rest of us at all?

It is possible to consider alternatives to Dickinson's narrative. Imagine we could re-write the scene immediately following the encounter with the spider from the perspective of another member of Li's tribe. I am going to invent such a creature. She will be another female whom I will call 'Le'. In my version of the story, Le has become worried by Li's absence and has followed her tracks to the tree, arriving shortly after Li has left. This is how my version of the story might continue:

> Le's attention was caught by a swift movement behind her. She looked down and saw a spider moving slowly across the earth. Le stared in fascination, all thoughts of Li driven momentarily from her mind. The spider was beautiful. Le's gaze eagerly acknowledged the cautious movements of its eight legs, the fragility of its tiny body. Suddenly, she found herself moving and turning in imitation of the little creature, twisting her arms and swaying her hips. Every time she moved, she made a tribute-sound in gratitude for the gift of the spider's beauty.

Howard Gardner (1993) has shown us that intelligence can manifest itself in different ways. These different kinds of intelligence can be placed into eight broad categories:

- naturalist
- interpersonal
- intrapersonal
- linguistic
- mathematical and logical
- visual and spatial
- kinesthetic
- musical

(Smith, 1998, p. 189).

Just as different people can extract different meanings from the same experience, so they may possess different forms of intelligence. One could argue, for example, that Li's dominant form of intelligence belongs to Gardner's 'mathematical and logical' category. The spider presents her with an intellectual puzzle. She 'assembles' her response to that puzzle as one might assemble the pieces of a jigsaw; and she uses the stimulus provided by the spider to create a functional tool. Le, on the other hand, could be regarded as someone for whom the 'kinesthetic' and 'musical' forms are most prominent. Her response to the spider is to dance and sing for joy. Of course, the model is not as crude as it might seem from this description. We all possess a mixture of all eight forms of intelligence. Both Li and Le, for example, make use of their 'visual and spatial' capacity, albeit for different ends. If we accept Gardner's theories, we have to acknowledge that the consequences for the ways in which we organize learning in our societies are profound.

Just as there are different kinds of intelligence, so there are different kinds of learning behaviours and objectives. An influential attempt to categorize these was made over 50 years ago by Bloom and others (Bloom *et al.*, 1956). Bloom envisaged a spectrum of intellectual endeavour which ranged from simple and factual to complex and conceptual. Starting with 'knowledge' and ascending to 'evaluation', the six categories are:

Knowledge
Comprehension
Application
Analysis
Synthesis

Evaluation
(Slavin, 1991, pp. 213–14).

Bloom and his colleagues do not suggest that we progress in a linear fashion upwards through the levels. Rather, we can operate at different points of the spectrum simultaneously. Again, Li offers a clear illustration of this. In the opening section of the quoted passage from Dickinson's novel, we can see her drawing upon 'knowledge' and 'evaluation' – the lowest and highest levels respectively – at the same time. When Li gazes into the unknown hinterland, she uses 'knowledge' (her ability to recall information) to orientate herself:

Before her lay the marsh. From the shore it had seemed endless, but now beyond it she saw a wavering line of blue, rising to peaks from two of which thin trails of smoke drifted skyward. She recognized them because there was another such peak at the centre of the island.

Li has to make a value judgement about this new landscape: 'The fifty miles or so of island shore which was the tribe's territory was all she had ever known, all the world there was.' As we have seen, her tribal teaching would have told her to shun this new landscape as unknown and potentially threatening. Instead, she draws upon Bloom's most complex level of objective – 'evaluation' – to go against the tribe's norms and to make her own, radically new, judgement about what she sees: 'Li stared entranced at the view. . .. Now, over there beyond the marshes, she saw another world, immense.'

Li also operates at high conceptual levels in certain areas and lower ones in others. Having observed the spider, for example, she demonstrates the ability to use 'application' (the capacity for applying principles or abstractions to problem-solving). She understands that she can use a grass stem as a mechanism for triggering the web's fall, that water can make grass pliable and that gourd-fibre possesses more of the durable qualities of spider thread than grass does. 'Analysis' (the capacity for breaking down complex information or ideas into simpler parts in order to understand how the parts are related or organized) comes into play when Li works out the reason why the dried grass stems kept breaking when she tried to weave them into a mesh. More fundamentally, she uses analytical skills to make her major conceptual breakthough – the perception that there could be a connection between web and shrimping-net:

There were two pictures in her mind – the minnows in the pool and the web dropping from the twigs. Northward there were rock-pools with minnows in them. A yellow one was especially delicious, but almost impossible to catch. But if she could make a web . . .

With her invention of the net and her first successful trawl of shrimps, Li achieves 'synthesis' – the creation of something that did not exist before – and humanity takes a major step along the road towards the world we know today.

Even while Li is achieving at these higher conceptual levels, she still finds herself struggling with 'comprehension' (the ability to translate, interpret and extrapolate information) which Bloom locates towards the simpler end of the spectrum. When she stared into the hinterland, she felt fear but 'didn't know what there was to be afraid of' since the only enemy she knows about is the shark, an aquatic creature. Later, we are told that she understands neither how the spider's web is made nor what triggered its fall; and when she first tries to bind the brittle grasses into a mesh, her fingers didn't understand why she could not weave them together.

Jerome Bruner (1960, 1966a, 1966b) offers a different perspective on Li's behaviour. Bruner does not focus, as Bloom and Gardner do, on the diversity of learning objectives and intelligences which are called into play whenever human beings respond to an intellectual challenge. Instead, he is more interested in thinking about learning as a means by which we represent the environment to ourselves. Bruner suggests that all our attempts at representation – no matter how diverse and complex they might seem – take place in three distinct stages, proceeding from the 'enactive' through the 'iconic' to the 'symbolic'.

Bruner's model can also help us to make sense of Li's learning behaviour. So much of what she achieves here is gained through 'learning by doing' – Bruner's first or 'enactive' stage. Thus, Li watches and imitates the spider; precipitates the web's fall by conducting her experiment with the grass stem. Notice the number of active verbs which Dickinson uses to describe her behaviour: 'she collected the longest stems'; 'she scooped away the burning surface'; 'she went and searched the dunes'. These 'enactive' behaviours help to lay effective foundations for Li's learning; but in order to make real inroads into understanding, she has to move on to the second stage, that of 'iconic representation'. This involves the ability to make connections between images and patterns. By internalizing those images and patterns, we can store experiences in our memory and draw upon them whenever we need to make sense of our environment in new ways. Consider how Dickinson describes Li's crucial, life-changing first encounter with the spider: Li uses the stored memory of a minnow darting through a pool to make sense of her encounter with a new creature – the spider. Their shared quality of speed establishes in her mind a connection between the two of them. This idea of connection is planted like a seed in her brain. It is as though spider and minnow represent two ends of a chain: Li feels impelled to link them in some way. The minnow represents something else in Li's memory-bank: food: 'Northward there were rock-pools with minnows in them. A yellow one was especially delicious, but almost impossible to catch.'

If spider and minnow are connected by the one picture, why should they not also be connected by the other? It is almost like a mathematical equation: 'spider plus something equals minnow'. The 'something' – the missing link in the chain – is the shrimping-net:

> There were two pictures in her mind – the minnows in the pool and the web dropping from the twigs. Northward there were rock-pools with minnows in them. A yellow one was especially delicious, but almost impossible to catch. But if she could make a web . . . How . . . ? With what . . . ?

Imagine that Li had a different picture to represent speed stored in her memory. Say, for example, the line in which she encounters the spider ran like this: 'Then a flick of movement caught her eye, speed followed by stillness, like a flash of lightning followed by the silence that comes before the thunder.' The 'equation' would then have been: 'spider plus something equals lightning'. Who knows what would have been the consequence of forging an intellectual chain between those two concepts? The 'learning outcome' is unlikely to have been a shrimping-net.

This brings us to the most important point of all. What crucially distinguishes Li from the spider is her capacity to internalize the insect's behaviour and to reproduce it in symbolic form. The spider can do no more than weave a physical web. Li can imitate its actions physically – by weaving together gourd-fibres, for example. More than this, however, she also possesses the uniquely human ability to 'weave an intellectual web' – patiently to spin threads of connection between the seemingly disconnected and disparate images stored in her memory. This ability places Li at the third and most sophisticated of Bruner's three levels – 'symbolic representation'. The fact that we possess the capacity to 'let one thing stand for another' is the 'psychological factor which transforms human learning' (Baumann *et al.*, 1997, p. 72). It opens the door to all those conceptual worlds which have so enhanced the quality of our existence: mathematics, music, philosophy, art. Above all, it grants us the ability to use that supreme medium of symbolic representation – language. It is interesting that when Dickinson wants to describe Li's first attempt to link spider and minnow, he uses a simile: 'Then a flick of movement caught her eye, speed followed by stillness, like a minnow in a pool.' Our capacity to use the fundamental building-blocks of figurative language – metaphor, metonym and synecdoche – enables us not only to store and combine complex ideas in our minds but also to communicate them to others.

We have considered Li's learning behaviour in some detail; but we have still not solved the mystery of why she, out of all her tribe, was the one to invent the shrimping-net. What was her motivation? Maslow (1954) can offer us some help here. He suggested that human beings have a hierarchy of needs. These needs can be represented symbolically by a pyramid. Starting from the 'base' and working upwards, these are:

- Physiological needs
- Safety needs
- Belongingness and love needs
- Esteem needs
- Need to know and understand
- Aesthetic needs
- Self-actualization needs

(Slavin, 1991, p. 321).

Maslow describes the lowest four as 'deficiency needs', in that, by satisfying them, we are seeking to remedy some perceived lack in ourselves. The top three are described as 'growth needs' because, Maslow suggests, they are goals we set ourselves once we feel whole and confident enough in ourselves to aspire intellectually, emotionally and spiritually.

'Necessity', we are told, 'is the mother of invention'; but if we apply Maslow's ideas to Li's behaviour, we will notice that the maxim does not appear to hold good in this case. Li is not driven to make the shrimping-net by a desperate need to eat. On the contrary, we are told that, at the time of her encounter with the spider, she is not hungry. Significantly, her moment of inspiration comes in the night, when she is resting. She chooses to conduct her experiment with the grass stems at evening, when the heat of the sun is not so fierce – and she scoops a cool hollow in the sand for herself, so that she may work more comfortably. The point is that learning seems to take place when our basic needs – the bottom 'layers' of Maslow's 'pyramid' – have been satisfied. Li is able to focus all her energy upon the spider because there is nothing else competing for her attention at the time. She has the tribe to thank for this. They have taught her how to catch shrimps and they have provided her with the sense of security which emboldens her to venture out to the tree. We could say that, by providing the 'foundations' of Maslow's 'pyramid', the tribe has enabled Li to progress from 'deficiency' to 'growth' needs. Dickinson makes it clear that Li is operating here at the level which Maslow terms the 'need to know and understand': 'But first she needed to know what the spider was up to. There was no reason for the need, no purpose or use in knowing. It was the mere knowledge that mattered.'

Earlier on in this chapter, I suggested that Li had three choices as to what she might do with her newly acquired knowledge about the shrimping-net. Having brought her tribe back into the story, it is time now to describe the third option – the one, in fact, which Dickinson has her choose. The extract from this passage ends:

> She hadn't intended to use it [the mesh of gourd-fibres] to catch shrimps – she could do that with her hands – and only wanted to see how the mesh worked, but at her first trawl she found several transparent bodies wriggling on the net. Delicately she picked them out, calling *Come-and-see* to Ma-ma.

Li decides to share her new-found knowledge with her tribe. By making this choice, she moves her learning from a personal into a social context. This in turn opens up complex issues, not only of morality, but of politics, also. Once learning enters the social arena, it becomes inextricably linked with questions of teaching, assessment and the nature of schooling. I shall consider these issues in my next chapter in this book (Chapter 4).

Response to 'How and Why do We Learn?'

Ian Gregory

Nick McGuinn's chapters (the one you have just read and the next chapter) are good examples of how imaginative literature in the hands of a skilled interpreter can be plundered (as it were) to introduce educational issues and concerns of deep importance in a manner far removed from the more prosaic approaches typifying writings on educational matters. Nick McGuinn's approach makes a welcome and stimulating change. In this brief response I will explore how far Li's learning experience (LLE) can aid us in understanding better, characteristic features of learning in a society such as ours that looks to schooling (in the main) to deliver education to its citizens.

Li is bent on exploration of the world around her. In the course of her wanderings beyond the world with which she is familiar she has experiences on the basis of which she makes connections, draws inferences, makes discoveries, creates an object flowing from her new understandings, and moves to share all she has found out with others. What is so singular about LLE is that she alone is involved in the learning episodes that have such significant outcomes. What is so striking about Li's adventure is how no-one else is directly involved in the discovery made. There is no teacher to be seen offering guidance, making suggestions, setting things up, all with a view to encouraging certain (largely) predetermined learning outcomes. This is a peculiarly undiluted form of learning by discovery.

Li's discovery is one fraught with particular significance. It is born of the desire (the need) to know and understand: '. . . she needed to know what the spider was up to. There was no reason for the need, no purpose or use in knowing. It was the mere knowledge that mattered.' Even as her efforts to use grass stems in making a web came to nothing, still 'she remained, absorbed. The failures them-selves were knowledge, feeding her need.' And Nick McGuinn himself attaches overwhelming significance to Li's coming to know by comparing Li to both Eve and Prometheus as examples of those who were prepared to risk everything for the sake of knowledge. Whilst being conscious of the humble nature of Li's construction of a fishing net as against the defiance of the gods by Prometheus and the challenging of sacred taboos, there is a similarity between the two in that in both instances, as Nick McGuinn puts it, 'learning takes place within a moral context and has moral consequences'. Once we possess knowledge it cannot be denied, all sorts of possi-bilities are now open to us which previously were not in our power. Rather like the genie, knowledge cannot be put back in the bottle. The important question now becomes what to do with the knowl-edge now in our hands. The momentous nature of Li's discovery resides so Nick McGuinn suggests in the fact that if Li had not discovered how to make the shrimping-net we would not now be living in a world in which our seas are being plundered of fish as trawlers hoover the sea-bed for their harvest.

What are we to make of all of this? Learning is central to human affairs. The question is; how far is the story of Li useful to us as we reflect upon the nature of learning generally and more particularly in our schools as educational institutions?

Comment has already been made on the individualistic nature of Li's learning: it involves her, the environment, the experiences had, the thought processes gone through, the making of the net conse-quent upon all the foregoing. Attention has been drawn to the sheer significance of what was discovered. A certain scepticism, however, is in order about LLE if our concern is with the kind of learning occurring every day in the lives of the innumerable human beings in our and every other society there has ever been and will be. And this scepticism becomes even more pointed if we concentrate on the typical efforts of schools and universities to educate their students. Great discoveries are made, they do transform our lives. There are individuals of great talent and insight who achieve breakthroughs, intellectual and creative, who put the rest of us in their debt. It is in the nature of some of those accomplishments that they can be put to the most fruitful or destructive of uses. Great scientific advance characteristically contains the potential for both substantial good and substantial harm. Nick McGuinn is right to highlight how ambivalent our attitude can be to certain of our advances in knowledge and understanding. At such times, we confront and are perplexed by the ethical dilemmas we clearly perceive as arising from the possibilities generated by the new knowledge and understanding we now possess. At the present time, for instance, the huge advances in genetic science following on from the breaking of the DNA code are a matter of considerable moral agitation. It is a frequent lament that humanity's advance in knowledge and understanding is not paralleled and matched by a corresponding advance in moral wisdom. But we mislead ourselves if we think that LLE is typical of the vast bulk of learning that goes on in all of our lives. Discovery (in the sense of finding out something for the first time of profound significance for humans) is very much the exception rather than the rule. Most of what we learn is already known by large numbers of people, has been known for a long time and is of varying degrees of significance, intrinsically, socially, and for individual lives. How we come to learn all these (kinds of) things is very varied, what we have learnt is enormously diverse, and our motivation in learning is not all of a piece for all individuals.

Let us flesh out a little these rather bare observations. All of us by accident of birth are born into a particular society distinguished by its social habits and customs, its religious culture, its cultural and political traditions and its stage of technological development. All societies take upon themselves the task of initiating their members into those traditions, customs and practices. In so-called advanced technological societies – and increasingly in all societies aspiring to such status – education is explicitly provided by agencies set up for the purpose. Education serves both individual and social purposes: the individual is granted access to the kinds of knowledge and understanding necessary to flourish in society, society is sustained by individuals equipped with the skills – intellectual, artistic, moral and practical – necessary to make a contribution to the welfare of society itself. These commonplace observations highlight what is surely true: that the vast bulk of what we have learnt, we learn from others. We are the inheritors of the learning of previous generations. *Learning, in short, is essentially a social enterprise.*

It is important to understand just what is meant by such an assertion. It is not simply that what there is to be learnt comes down to us because of the strivings and genius of previous generations of human beings, that all there is to learn is dependent on what other have accomplished. More fundamentally, someone who has learnt successfully is an individual who has come to satisfy the criteria defining success in some relevant area. What constitutes successful learning is having satisfied the requirements associated with some rule-governed activity. The rules are publicly ascertainable, the criteria of successful learning are publicly understood and shared by members of the community. To have learnt the two times table is to demonstrate through verbal behaviour and associated manipulations of objects that the learner has measured up to those rules defining multiplication by two. To have learnt the rules of grammar is to be able to demonstrate a facility with words that satisfies the social practice of writing in a socially countenanced manner. To not be able to make the next move in multiplication by two or to have no idea how to use the full stop is, contrariwise, to demonstrate a failure of learning – a failure of learning evidenced by the inability to measure up to what the rules governing such activities demand. All learning involves measuring up to the public standards defining success across the diverse range of human activities.

The requirement that learning always takes place in the context of social practices – of a bewildering diversity, of course – also brings to the fore another consideration of great importance: that in the main those who learn are influenced hugely by others who in various ways promote and encourage their learning. The precise relationship between learning and the agents and factors that influence learning is a complex and much discussed issue. Foremost among those issues is the precise nature of the relationship between teaching and learning. Is teaching necessarily to be defined in terms of the intention to produce learning? Is learning the invariable outcome of teaching? What seems certainly true of anyone who has learnt anything (can satisfy the appropriate criteria defining success in whatever area) is that their success in satisfying the relevant criteria should not simply be due to maturation, something occurring 'by the light of nature', as it were. If an insect can fly immediately upon birth, it has not learnt to fly; if it immediately seeks out a mate whatever is happening, this is not a matter of learned behaviour. If we could talk with our customary fluency at birth there would be no such thing as having to learn our first language. Indeed, there is a body of opinion which thinks that first language acquisition is not a genuine form of learning at all. The comparison with learning a second language is instructive. A process of learning is gone through, we rely upon others to aid us in mastery of what is not our native tongue. There are public criteria of having mastered written and conversational French (say) that we aspire to and which are the measure of how successful our learning of the French language is.

It is not to the point to characterize in great detail exactly what it is to learn. But it is worth remembering that learning can go on in the absence of another explicitly setting him or herself to try and encourage, promote another in the learning of some bit of information, practice of some skill, the achievement of some excellence. One can learn things incidentally, in passing, by accident, despite oneself, reluctantly and so on and so on. Famously Aristotle thought virtue was 'caught, not taught'. There seem to be other occasions where we are moved to say that someone taught us all we know in circumstances in which it was never part of *their* intention that we learn anything at all. As a keen tennis player I developed a lethal topspin backhand by watching the great Australian Rod Laver plying his trade on the tennis court and seeking to emulate his example. As a decent human being treating other humans with respect, others might claim me as their moral mentor, impressed as they might be by how I treat others. One could multiply such examples almost endlessly. All of us owe something to someone who unknown to themselves taught us something important we have incorporated into our lives. In these instances, justifiably or not, we seem to hold the other person – the object of our attention and admiration – *responsible* for what we have learnt. Presumably the innocent other would never conceive of themselves as teachers in the primary sense in which to be a teacher of maths (say) is to be someone who engages in activities intended to produce appropriate knowledge of maths. Be that as it may, the key point to cling on to is that whatever it is to learn, however it is learning comes about, the whole process takes place within a social world; a social world that in the nature of things most of the time involves others in the promotion of learning and which always through the rules governing human activities and accomplishments determines what is going to count as successful learning.

Why LLE (whatever Nick McGuinn's considered views on the foregoing issues) might not be a good exemplar to be guided by is that learning is represented as too much of an individual triumph – both in terms of how the learning occurred and in the very significance of what was learnt. Almost all of what we have learnt, are learning and will learn is rooted in social interactions of one kind or another. Almost all of what we ever learn is from others and is a far cry from the kind of discovery Li made. Not only is what we characteristically learn derivative and second hand, vast amounts of what we learn is small fry and of no great moment.

What is true generally is, we feel tempted to say, peculiarly true of schooling. This is not to say that what we learn at schools is not important. It is of the most profound importance. Education is the selective transmission of a given society's culture. It represents the 'initiation' of the coming generation into that culture. Judgements are made about what elements of that culture are so important that their transmission and furtherance should not be left to chance. We have schools employing individuals called teachers whose job is to bring the young to a stage where initiation into the culture has occurred. Teachers do that by engaging in activities intended to promote learning of the preferred kinds. If successful, individuals are able to pass their lives better within a given society. But what is learnt is not original, it is not pathbreaking, it is wholly dependent upon previous generations – not simply in its content but for its transmission. And consequential upon that, unlike Li's discovery of the net for landing shrimps, what is learnt is barely laden with moral significance.

Most of what we have said seems almost platitudinous. These observations are of a highly general nature. Nothing has been said about how to encourage learning within the school context. Teachers have at their disposal a whole battery of techniques they might use to excite interest in what they wish to see learnt. In this connection it is worth mentioning that the ability to excite interest as a mark of a good teacher rather suggests that Li may be relatively unusual in being driven by the desire to know. To rely upon such motivation to advance learning may be rewarded but will as frequently not be. One of the tasks of the teacher trainer is to acquaint the would-be teacher with the variety of ways of encouraging learning that experience has demonstrated can aid the development of learning. We know (and Nick McGuinn correctly draws our attention to the fact) that given the different manifestations of intelligence and the range of different experiences individuals bring to a learning situation, the very same situation might spark off different responses in terms of what is learnt. The competent teacher will be sensitive to the particularities of the children he or she is teaching and encouraging to learn – their different backgrounds, their different talents, their different partialities. And he or she will conduct him or herself appropriately. Indeed it is these kinds of considerations along with the bewildering variety of things to be learnt that should make us suspicious of the possibilities of using some preferred learning theory (e.g. constructivism, behaviourism) as the template for how we should conduct ourselves as teachers. We have to hand a wealth of folk wisdom, born of the endless task of seeking to promote learning in our educational agencies, not easily to be set aside because of an undue deference to grand theorizing about the learning process. It is as well to remind ourselves that grand theorizing starts from what we already know about how to encourage learning. There is no reason to suppose that the varieties of learning we seek to encourage through schooling should be amenable to one particular preferred way of teaching rooted in a preferred learning theory. Our folk wisdom in these matters is much better grounded empirically than the grand theories of learning competing for our attention.

Of course there is such a thing as 'learning by discovery'. Of course, each one of us as a learner has, quite unproblematically, 'discovered' things for ourselves. But what we have discovered is not new. It might be new *to us* and the fact we have discovered it for ourselves might render what we have learnt of more significance to us than much else we have learnt because someone has told us what we now know. In the context of schooling, however, what we discover most of the time is what it was always intended we should 'discover'. Rousseau in the most important text in the history of educational thought *Emile* (1911) envisages Emile learning everything via learning from discovery and via learning from experience. Emile never has the sensation of being *made* to learn anything. But the reality is that whatever Emile learns is what the tutor wants him to learn. The tutor has connived to set up circumstances eventuating in the learning on Emile's part – learning the tutor always intended should occur. Even in the greatest of the child-centred texts, the teacher holds the key to the promotion and direction of the most significant learning.

What has been suggested is that the best place to begin understanding the nature of learning is by recognizing the essentially social and co-operative nature of the learning process. The example of Li, while correctly emphasizing how what we are able to learn is a function of our previous experiences and beliefs, encourages an unduly romantic nature of the individual striving for and achieving learning through the exercise of remarkable powers. Except in the limiting instances of those who are blessed by making great breakthroughs in whatever area it be, the reality for the rest of us is altogether more prosaic. And even in the case of the great innovators, they achieve on the back of others. The great creative leaps come to those already well versed in what has gone before. This reality is nicely captured in the adage about genius being 99 per cent perspiration, 1 per cent inspiration, and the related idea that it is the well-prepared mind that achieves the breakthrough.

Education (and schooling) have as their ambition the introduction of the next generation to the accomplishments and achievements of human beings in a given society at a given time. The range of humanity's accomplishments and achievements are many and varied. Judgements are made as to what is of most worth. The task of education is to transmit something of that which is deemed most worthwhile. To that end, we teach so that those we teach may learn. In coming to learn they embrace the activities and practices informing so much that makes our lives worthwhile. The learning that goes on is irredeemably social; both in terms of others (teachers) accepting responsibility for promoting that learning and in that the measure of whether learning has successfully occurred is a matter of public record (processes of *assessment* testifying that certain public criteria defining success have been satisfied). We can admire those who have insights denied the rest of us but they are as much the beneficiaries of those who taught them as any of the rest of us. The sustaining of our culture is not through the activities of heroic individuals but in the endless small instances of teachers teaching and learners learning. As ever, it is mankind working collaboratively and co-operatively that marks the way forward. In the endeavour to advance learning, the teacher as a custodian of our culture has a necessary role to play.

Activities

In Chapter 2, I try to explore some of the ways in which human beings learn and the motives which inspire that learning. Ian Gregory, in his response to the chapter, argues that my account places too much emphasis upon those rare, life-changing moments of conceptual breakthrough which, he believes, represent the exception rather than the rule of human learning. Mistrustful of such 'romantic' accounts of human progress, Ian Gregory asserts the essentially social nature of education: 'Education is the selective transmission of a given society's culture. It represents the "initiation" of the coming generation into that culture.' Much of the transmission process is, he says, of necessity, 'derivative', 'second hand' and 'of no great moment'. 'As ever,' Ian Gregory concludes, 'it is mankind working collaboratively and co-operatively that marks the way forward.'

Outlined below are a number of key questions related to my chapter and Ian Gregory's response to it. They are accompanied by a number of assertions (marked out as bullet points below) which are designed to help you to explore your response to the questions.

Key Questions

To what extent can learning be described as a social enterprise?

- Ways of classifying experience are social constructs, not natural phenomena.
- Society decides which experiences are worth studying and which not.
- Society sets the rules for judging whether learning has been successful or not.
- We learn what we are meant to learn.
- Individuals who make a significant contribution to human understanding build upon a foundation of 'second hand' knowledge.
- Learners need to be prepared to take risks by breaking with tradition and defying social convention.
- Every act of learning has social and moral consequences.

How and why do we learn?

- Necessity is the mother of invention.
- We learn most effectively when we feel secure and content.
- Failure is an essential part of the learning process.
- Individuals can be intelligent in different ways.
- No one learning style can suit everybody.
- The capacity for symbolic representation is the key to successful learning.

Suggestions for Reading

Bruner, J. S. (1960) *The Process of Education*. Cambridge, Mass.: Harvard University Press.

Bruner, J. S. (1966) *A Study of Thinking*. Chichester: Wiley.

Bruner, J. S. (1966) *Towards a Theory of Instruction*. New York: Norton. Like Piaget, Bruner believes that 'mistakes' can provide valuable insights into understanding. He argues that language is the fundamental tool of learning and that the kinds of thinking strategies we use depend upon the context in which the learning takes place, our knowledge and the materials at our disposal. Bruner defines three stages by which we represent the environment to ourselves when we are learning: the enactive, the iconic and the symbolic.

Donaldson, M. (1978) *Children's Minds*. London: Fontana.

Donaldson, M. (1992) *Human Minds: An Exploration*. London: Penguin Books. Donaldson is influenced by and critical of Piaget's theories concerning the development of knowledge. She stresses the need to consider the whole person in the learning process. She also explores the reasons why some enthusiastic young learners lose interest in education when they reach secondary school. By way of explanation, she focuses upon the tensions between 'human sense' and 'disembedded thought'.

Gardner, H. (1993) *Frames of Mind: The Theory of Multiple Intelligences*. New York: Basic Books. Read Gardner's account of his theory for yourself, see how his ideas might have a practical application, and consider possible criticisms of his work (e.g. Smith and White (see below)).

Slavin, R. E. (1991) *Educational Psychology: Theory into Practice*. Boston and London: Allyn & Bacon. This text makes a particularly useful starting-point because Slavin offers a comprehensive and lucid account of a wide variety of learning issues. Particularly helpful is the way in which he locates theory within a practical context. The sections of his text most relevant to this chapter are those which describe (and criticize) the work of Bloom, Bruner, Maslow and Piaget.

Smith, A. (1998) *Accelerated Learning in Practice: Brain-based Methods for Accelerating Motivation and Achievement*. Stafford: Network Educational Press.

White, J. (2000) *Do Howard Gardner's Multiple Intelligences Add Up?* London: Institute of Education.

Suggested Practical Activities

1. Review your history as a learner. Think of a time when you felt that you made a breakthrough in understanding – perhaps it was when you learnt to swim or to ride a bicycle. It is important that the experience you choose should *not* have taken place in a school or college classroom. Focus upon your chosen moment. Using Maslow's 'Hierarchy' as a guide, explore the motives behind your learning. Compare your experiences with others.

2. Now repeat the activity, this time choosing a moment from your school or college experience. What similarities or differences do you notice? What conclusions do you draw from this?

3. Think of a time when you learnt from a mistake. What was it? How did you feel about it? How and why did the mistake advance your learning? If other people were aware of the mistake, how did they respond to it?

4. Think of an academic task you have been asked to perform recently – writing an essay, perhaps, or preparing a seminar

presentation. Using Bloom's *Taxonomy* as a framework, analyse in detail the learning challenges implicit in the task and describe how you intend to meet them.

5. Keep a record of all the learning experiences you encounter during a typical working day. Try to categorize your responses to these experiences according to Gardner's theory of multiple intelligences. Does the theory make sense? Is there an area that you excel in or one in which you seem to be less proficient? Are you using particular forms of intelligence in particular situations? Do you seem to have a preferred learning style? To what extent is your working environment allowing you to 'play to your strengths' – or not?

6. As an extension to the above activity, try 'shadowing' someone at work. Choose a person whose job is very different from your own. Compare your results with theirs.

7. Read what Margaret Donaldson has to say about 'human sense' and 'disembedded thought'. Visit a nursery or primary school and observe a group of children at work on a conceptual problem. How do they go about solving it? Do Donaldson's ideas offer helpful insights into what is taking place? Can you 'map' the children's progress according to Bruner's three stages of representation?

8. As an extension to this activity, compare the children's learning behaviour and the work they did with your own experiences at that age. Talk to somebody who was at primary school 30 or more years ago. How do the three sets of experience compare? How would you account for the similarities and/or the differences?

CHAPTER 3

Who Teaches and Why?

Nick McGuinn

At the end of my last chapter, we left our heroine, Li, calling on her mother to come and see the shrimping-net she had invented. Why does Li decide to share her newly acquired knowledge? Perhaps she feels a debt of gratitude to her tribe. Have they not, after all, been responsible for her schooling? This might seem an odd thing to say in relation to a story about prehistoric hominids who had no conception of classrooms or curricula. But if we recall that 'school' comes from the Ancient Greek word for 'leisure', the reference starts to make sense. Li's tribe have provided her with the 'leisure' to make her discovery by granting her freedom from the so-called 'deficiency needs' identified by Maslow and discussed in my earlier chapter. It is because Li feels well fed, and secure in the knowledge that her mother is within calling distance, that she has the intellectual, emotional and physical 'leisure' to concentrate upon the spider.

The same principle applies in education today. People engaged in study at school or college are – theoretically at least – granted the freedom to withdraw from the grind of daily life so that they can focus all their energies upon their studies. Societies which organize their education systems in this way do not act out of pure altruism. They feel that they are making an investment for the future. The students of today will 'pay' for their educational leisure by becoming the skilled and economically productive workers of tomorrow. Totalitarian regimes take this approach to its extreme by implementing what has been called a 'patriotic model' which demands, in return for educational leisure, nothing less than the total subjection of the students' interests to the interests of those who made that education possible (Rowe, 2000). But even pluralistic democracies expect a return on their investment. The quotation which follows is taken from the famous 'Ruskin Speech' of October 1976 in which the British Prime Minister of the day, James Callaghan, initiated his so-called 'Great Debate' on educational matters:

> I take it that no one claims exclusive rights in this field [of education]. Public interest is strong and legitimate and will be satisfied. We spend £6 billion a year on education, so there will be discussion. (Callaghan, 1976, p. 332)

Perhaps Li's decision to share her knowledge is motivated by a sense of obligation, a willingness to 'pay back' some at least of the prehistoric equivalent of Callaghan's £6 billion a year. It may be, however, that she is inspired by something deeper – a sense of priest-like vocation. The more the social structures of Britain were shaken by industrial, scientific and political change in the nineteenth century, for example, the more education was invested with an almost religious capacity to transform and redeem society. The liberal educationalist Henry Sidgwick argued in 1868 that 'the schoolmaster' ought to be nothing less than a 'missionary of culture' (Sidgwick, 1868, p. 106). Half a century later, in 1921, the Newbolt Report called upon the nation's teaching force to repair a social fabric grievously damaged by the ravages of the First World War:

> The judgements and experience laid before us by those who have a large experience and every right to express a judgement, support us in our belief that an education of this kind is the greatest benefit which could be conferred upon any citizen of a great state, and that the common right to it, the common discipline and enjoyment of it, the common possession of the tastes and associations connected with it, would form a new element of national unity, linking together the mental life of all classes by experiences which have hitherto been the privilege of a limited section. (Quoted in Crowley, 1991, pp. 197–8)

As Margaret Mathieson put it in her study of English and English teachers a quarter of a century ago:

> At every stage of the subject's growth, during which new hopes have been invested in it as a liberalising force, fresh demands

have been made for inspirational teachers. In response to what they have seen as a worsening cultural crisis, educationalists have recurrently called for exceptional teachers to face unsympathetic conditions in the schools and the 'forces' of modern urban society. (Mathieson, 1975, p. 12)

Any teacher who accepts this definition of their role takes a heavy burden upon themselves. The writer D. H. Lawrence is someone who, at the turn of the last century, accepted – and felt himself ultimately defeated by – the challenge. In his famous poem 'Afternoon: The Last Lesson' (in De Sola Pinto and Roberts, 1964), he likens the experience of teaching to a fire which, if left unchecked, will consume body and soul. Faced by a class of 'unruly' pupils, he realizes that he is not prepared to pay this price:

> And shall I take
> The last dear fuel and heap it on my soul
> Till I rouse my will like a fire to consume
> Their dross of indifference, and burn the scroll
> Of their insults in punishment? – I will not!
> I will not waste myself to embers for them,
> Not all for them shall the fires of my life be hot,
> For myself a heap of ashes of weariness, till sleep
> Shall have raked the embers clear: I will keep
> Some of my strength for myself, for if I should sell
> It all for them, I should hate them –
> – I will sit and wait for the bell.

Lawrence's image of all-consuming fire is an apt one. It conveys something of the intense, almost charismatic, effort of will required by the teacher who wishes to impart new knowledge to students who either will not or do not know how to receive it.

'Familiarity', the old saying goes, 'breeds contempt.' We leave work one evening and notice that the weather is misty. We register the fact as a minor irritation – perhaps it will delay our homeward journey – and then hurry on, thinking no more of it. We've experienced mist countless times before. We know, from the dictionary, that it is only: 'a water vapour near the ground in minute droplets limiting visibility' (*The Oxford Compact English Dictionary* (Thompson, D. (ed.), 1996). And then along comes a poet like Craig Raine who, in his poem 'A Martian Sends a Postcard Home' (Raine, 1979), seems to slam the dictionary shut. To him:

> Mist is when the sky is tired of flight
> and rests its soft machine on ground
> then the world is dim and bookish
> like engravings under tissue paper.

Why is Craig Raine's definition of mist so different from the one in the dictionary? T. S. Eliot, a fellow poet, would say it was because human beings cannot bear much reality. It is easier to keep one's head down than to look up, to acquiesce rather than to question, to accept rather than to defy convention. According to the seventeenth-century philosopher John Locke, words themselves – the very stuff of communication – are actually used to deny rather than to embrace reality:

> when we would consider, or make propositions about . . . more complex ideas, as of a *man, vitriol, fortitude, glory*, we usually put the name for the idea: because the ideas these names stand for, being for the most part imperfect, confused, and undetermined, we reflect on the names themselves, because they are more clear, certain, and distinct, and readier occur to our thoughts than the pure ideas: and so we make use of these words instead of the ideas themselves, even when we would meditate and reason within ourselves, and make tacit mental propositions. (Quoted in Canfield and Donnell, 1964, p. 258)

Rather than open ourselves up to all the possible meanings – frightening, exhilarating or whatever – that the concept of 'mist' might hold for our lives, we prefer to neutralize it, to make it safe by containing it within a neat and unproblematic dictionary definition. And if we are prepared to do that with a relatively 'safe' concept like 'mist', what are we to do with more challenging ideas like 'freedom', 'love' – or 'education'?

To refuse to face up to the challenge of reality in this way, Jerome Bruner argues, is to risk atrophy: 'What does not change ceases to register: steady states in their very nature cease to stimulate' (Bruner, 1971, p. 4). The fundamental task of the teacher is to challenge complacency, to shatter preconceptions, to make the familiar strange. Bruner continues:

> There is compelling evidence that so long as the environment conforms to the expected patterns within reasonable limits, alerting mechanisms in the brain are quietened. But once expectancy is violated, once the world ceases strikingly to

correspond to our models of it . . . then all the alarms go off
and we are at full alertness . . . (Bruner, 1971, p. 5)

The twentieth-century radical Brazilian educationalist Paolo Freire
offers an overtly political interpretation of the ideas expounded here
by Locke and Bruner. He argues that it is not enough to read 'the
word'. One must also 'read the world' which is represented or (as
Locke might put it) obscured by that word (Freire and Macedo,
1987). Freire's colleague, Donaldo Macedo, provides an example of
what this might mean in practice:

This [the capacity to read both 'the word' and 'the world']
implies, obviously, the ability, for example, of medical special-
ists in the United States who have contributed to a great
technological advancement in medicine to understand and
appreciate why over 30 million Americans do not have access
to this medical technology and why we still have the highest
infant mortality rate in comparison to other developed nations.
(Macedo, 1994, pp. xvii–xviii)

To 'violate expectancy', to bring people to a state of 'full alertness'
by making 'all the alarms go off', in Bruner's words: in order to
accomplish these things, one must have the vision to see the possible
behind the actual. One must possess the courage to face the truth,
no matter how unpalatable it might be. One must have the strength
of will not only to defy convention but also to imagine and to
implement change. Qualities such as these equate the teacher's role
with that of the poet, the prophet, the revolutionary, the visionary.
This is the awesome figure whose voice booms out from the Introduction to William Blake's *Songs of Innocence and Experience* (Ostriker, 1977) in 1794:

> Hear the voice of the bard,
> Who present, past and future sees –
> Whose ears have heard
> The Holy Word
> That walked among the ancient trees . . .

William Shakespeare recognized this figure, too. In his portrayal
of Prospero, the scholar-magician from *The Tempest* (1611–12) he
presents a supreme manifestation of the teacher as awe-inspiring
visionary. As the play draws to a climax in Act V, Prospero recounts
his powers in language more suited to a god than a human being:

> I have bedimm'd
> The noontide sun, call'd forth the mutinous winds,
> And 'twixt the green sea and the azur'd vault
> Set roaring war: to the dread rattling thunder
> Have I given fire and rifted Jove's stout oak
> With his own bolt; the strong-bas'd promontory
> Have I made shake, and by the spurs pluck'd up
> The pine and cedar: graves at my command
> Have wak'd their sleepers, op'd, and let 'em forth
> By my so potent Art.
> (*The Tempest*, V. i. 41–50)

Figures such as Blake's Bard or Shakespeare's Prospero have the calibre, surely, to meet the stern challenges set by Locke, Bruner and Freire. If the classrooms of the world were peopled by teachers such as these, life might indeed be radically transformed! But would this necessarily be a good thing? The capacity to 'violate expectancy' can cause harm – as it does in *The Tempest*. Prospero and his daughter Miranda, having been exiled from the city-state of Milan, are cast ashore upon an island inhabited by, amongst others, a 'salvage [*sic*] and deformed slave' (Quoted in Kermode, 1964, p. 2) called Caliban. Savage and deformed Caliban may be; but he loves his island home. When the newcomers make friendly overtures to him, his first impulse is to respond with generosity. By the time we join the play here in Act I Scene ii, however, relationships between the three have broken down irretrievably. Caliban curses the fact that he is no longer the host but the prisoner of his former guests:

> All the charms
> Of Sycorax, toads, beetles, bats, light on you!
> For I am all the subjects that you have,
> Which first was mine own King; and here you sty me
> In this hard rock, whiles you do keep from me
> The rest o' th' island.
> (*The Tempest*, I. ii. 341–6)

Prospero and Miranda's response to Caliban's invective is worth quoting at some length because it shows just how and why 'expectancy' might be 'violated' to harmful effect. Prospero replies first:

> Thou most lying slave,
> Whom stripes may move, not kindness! I have us'd thee,
> Filth as thou art, with human care; and lodg'd thee

> In mine own cell, till thou didst seek to violate
> The honour of my child.
> (*The Tempest*, I. ii. 346–50)

Far from rejecting this charge, Caliban welcomes it:

> O ho, O ho! would't had been done!
> Thou didst prevent me; I had peopled else
> This isle with Calibans.
> (*The Tempest*, I. ii. 351–3)

Understandably, the sound of her would-be rapist boasting about his crime is too much for Miranda to bear. She joins in the attack:

> Abhorred slave,
> Which any print of goodness wilt not take,
> Being capable of all ill! I pitied thee,
> Took pains to make thee speak, taught thee each hour
> One thing or other: when thou didst not, savage,
> Know thine own meaning, but wouldst gabble like
> A thing most brutish, I endow'd thy purposes
> With words that made them known. But thy vile race,
> Though thou didst learn, had that in't which good natures
> Could not abide to be with; therefore wast thou
> Deservedly confin'd into this rock,
> Who hadst deserv'd more than a prison.
> (*The Tempest*, I. ii. 353–64)

And then Caliban utters the famous words of defiance which have resonated throughout literature:

> You taught me language; and my profit on't
> Is, I know how to curse. The red plague rid you
> For learning me your language!
> (*The Tempest*, I. ii. 365–7)

I do not wish to condone Caliban's behaviour here. However, I think it is fair to say that Prospero and Miranda are not entirely blameless. What, for example, gave them the right to assume that their host on the island was an inferior being in need of the benefits of their educational system? Shakespeare makes it clear that, when the three first met, it was in fact Caliban who taught Prospero and Miranda what they needed to know in order to survive in their new environment. Caliban reminds them:

> then I lov'd thee,
> And show'd thee all the qualities o' th' isle,
> The fresh springs, brine-pits, barren place and fertile . . .
> (*The Tempest*, I. ii. 338–40)

He already possesses all the knowledge he needs to function perfectly well on the island.

In this next extract from the play, Caliban offers to help another new arrival called Stephano who has, incidentally, come from the same society as Prospero and Miranda and is even less well equipped to cope with the environment than they were. As Caliban reels off the list of foods he could offer his guest, he speaks with the easy fluency and authority of the expert:

> I prithee, let me bring thee where crabs grow;
> And I with my long nails will dig thee pig-nuts;
> Show thee a jay's nest, and instruct thee how
> To snare the nimble marmoset; I'll bring thee
> To clustering filberts, and sometimes I'll get thee
> Young scammels from the rocks.
> (*The Tempest*, II. ii. 167–72)

If we were to identify the skills revealed by Caliban in this speech according to the criteria of Howard Gardner's 'multiple intelligences' outlined in my earlier chapter, we might be surprised by the results. In four of Gardner's suggested areas at least, Caliban is clearly operating at a high level of sophistication. Perhaps most striking is his sense of *naturalist* intelligence. According to Alistair Smith, people who possess this quality:

> will be at home in and delight in the natural environment. An ability to describe the features of a natural environment and classify species will often be accompanied by a sense of elation at being there. (Smith, 1998, p. 184)

Caliban fits this description perfectly. He knows every inch of his island home, from seashore to forest; knows, too, when and where to harvest the bounties of Nature. What long hours of patient, absorbed concentration did he expend in order to track the jay to its nest or to learn how to outwit the 'nimble' marmoset?

Caliban possesses *kinesthetic* intelligence, too:

> Those with kinesthetic intelligence will have the ability to use the body in highly differentiated and skilled ways. To work with objects and manipulate them with finesse. They will learn

best by doing where physical movement aids memory. (Smith, 1998, p. 177)

Whether picking crab-apples from the trees, digging nuts from the ground, catching young sea-birds or snaring small mammals, Caliban is kinesthetically adept. And all these skills require the use of *visual and spatial* intelligence, which manifests itself in a capacity for: 'seeing and observing, visualising desired outcomes and some of the stages seen in working towards the successful achievement of that outcome' (Smith, 1998, p. 173).

Finally, there is Caliban's use of *mathematical and logical* intelligence:

Individuals with a mathematical and logical intelligence are problem-solvers who can construct solutions non-verbally. They delight in sequence, logic and order and can readily discern patterns and relationships in the world around them. (Smith, 1998, p. 167)

If Li demonstrates mathematical and logical skills when she invents her shrimping-net, how much more so does Caliban here. His marmoset snare is no clumsy prototype but a tried and tested, fully working model. And the problems solved in order to make it work were all overcome 'non-verbally' – for is not Caliban's lack of language one of the qualities for which Prospero and Miranda most despise him?

So much for Caliban the learner. How does he measure up as a teacher? Look closely again at the speech from Act II, scene ii quoted earlier. Note the pattern of verb phrases which he uses in those six lines: *bring thee, dig thee, show thee, instruct thee, get thee.* If the new guest, Stephano, is to survive on the island, he must learn by experiencing what Caliban has experienced and by doing what Caliban has done. Caliban's role as teacher is to 'show' rather than to 'tell'. If his teaching proves successful, Stephano will not starve to death.

By teaching in this way, Caliban is advocating a rather extreme version of the experiential approach to teaching and learning 150 years before its first great exponent, the French philosopher Jean Jacques Rousseau, wrote his defining work on the subject – *Emile* (1762). Compare Caliban's words about snaring marmosets and picking crab-apples to this description by Rousseau of the way in which a teacher might approach the subject of 'measuring, perceiving, and estimating distance':

There is a very tall cherry tree; how shall we gather the cherries? Will the ladder in the barn be big enough? There is a wide stream; how shall we get to the other side? Would one of the wooden planks in the yard reach from bank to bank? (Rousseau, 1911, p. 105)

Caliban's insistence that Stephano learns by doing links him as a teacher not only with Rousseau but also with the great exponents of 'discovery learning' in the twentieth century – Jean Piaget and Jerome Bruner.

There is a connection here, too, with another important twentieth century figure – Lev Vygotsky. The clue to that connection lies in Caliban's promise to 'instruct' Stephano how to 'snare the nimble marmoset'. One of Vygotsky's most important contributions to our thinking about education is his account of what is now known as 'the zone of proximal development'. Slavin describes it thus:

there are certain skills or understandings that students have mastered completely, others they are on the verge of mastering, and others that are beyond their present capacity to accommodate. [Vygotsky] argued that instruction should focus on those skills that students are 'on the verge' of learning, which he called the proximal zone of development. That is, the purpose of instruction is to gradually stretch students' understandings into new territory just beyond comfortable concepts. (Slavin, 1991, p. 39)

I doubt whether Caliban would have put it quite like this; but the principle behind his actions is the same. Caliban could have simply told Stephano that marmosets were good to eat and that it was possible to snare them – and then left his new companion either to puzzle out how it might be done or else starve to death. Instead, he is prepared to pass on his own hard-won knowledge and to save Stephano vital time by showing him what to do.

The kind of teacher Caliban represents here is very different from Sidgwick's 'missionary of culture', Blake's Bard or even Lawrence's 'burnt out' idealist. His approach to teaching is fundamentally egalitarian. Vygotsky would have wanted to investigate Stephano's zone of proximal development, to ascertain whether he was ready intellectually to be taught the intricacies of marmoset-snaring. Caliban, however, makes no judgements – academic, social or whatever – about his new pupil. Nor does he attach any conditions to his teaching. He does not try to sell it, nor to demand anything in return. He takes it for granted that Stephano is capable of learning and he is as willing to help him learn as he is to share his island home.

So what has happened to transform this apparently benevolent and skilful teacher and learner into a foul-mouthed, would-be rapist? A clue to the answer lies in Miranda's speech from Act 1, Scene ii of *The Tempest* quoted earlier. If we again trace the verb phrases used by the speaker, we find a pattern totally unlike the one revealed when Caliban's words were analysed in the same way: *I pitied thee . . . Took pains to make thee speak . . . I endow'd thy purposes . . . therefore wast thou/Deservedly confin'd into this rock. . . .* Miranda's words reveal a very different attitude towards teaching. She sees education as a favour bestowed by someone in power upon someone who is powerless. Miranda's teaching comes with conditions; and because Caliban does not abide by those conditions, he has to pay the forfeit of his liberty.

It is possible to interpret this confrontation between Caliban and Miranda as a manifestation of 'cultural imperialism' – the process by which one dominant group's experience and culture is 'universalized' and established as the norm for all other groups (Young, 1992, p. 191). Certainly, Henry Sidgwick would recognize Miranda as a teacher in the true 'missionary of culture' mould. Her mission is to spread the values of her culture through the medium of language. *Linguistic intelligence* is the only one of Howard Gardner's multiple intelligences that she recognizes. Because Caliban is weak in this area, Miranda fails to see his many strengths and therefore dismisses him as stupid. This is why her attacks upon Caliban focus upon his inability to speak:

> . . . when thou didst not, savage,
> Know thine own meaning, but wouldst gabble like
> A thing most brutish, I endow'd thy purposes
> With words that made them known.

If Miranda were not completely blinded by her obsession with the importance of language, she would have to admit that this statement is not true. Had Caliban really been incapable of 'knowing his own meaning', he would not have been able to live so successfully upon his island. Miranda's statement is not only inaccurate but also – in the way that it recalls the opening lines of The New Testament's *Gospel According to St. John* – extraordinarily egocentric. St John's Gospel begins:

In the beginning was the Word, and the Word was with God, and the Word was God.

The same was in the beginning with God.

All things were made by him; and without him was not any thing made that was made.
(St John 1: 1–3)

It is as though Miranda is equating herself with God. The implication of her statement is that Caliban's existence was devoid of meaning until she arrived on the island and 'endow'd' his 'purposes' with words. This is almost like saying that Caliban did not exist until Miranda 'created' him through language – a language that was completely beyond the realms of his own experience.

'The consequences for Caliban are dire. Victims of cultural imperialism 'live their oppression by viewing themselves from the perspective of the way others view them . . .' (McLaren and Lankshear, 1994, p. 5). This condition is known as 'double consciousness'. The victim of it 'desires recognition as human, capable of activity, full of hope and possibility, but receives from the dominant culture only the judgement that he or she is different, marked, or inferior' (Young, 1992, p. 191). This is precisely Caliban's predicament. Measured exclusively against Miranda's criterion of linguistic intelligence, his non-verbal skills count for nothing. All he can do is accept one of the two stereotypical positions of powerlessness which she offers him. He can either be patronized as a pathetic victim, or he can be demonized as a 'thing most brutish'. He chooses the latter – and it is a testimony to his fighting spirit that he does so.

To a Marxist critic like Louis Althusser, the model of teaching offered here by Miranda might serve as a powerful example of the way in which a capitalist state uses education to embed the ideology of the ruling class within the society it controls. What takes place on Caliban's island, Althusser would suggest, is in fact no different from what takes place on a daily basis in the classrooms of the capitalist world (Althusser, 1972b).

Other radical commentators, such as Paulo Freire and his followers, might locate Miranda's model of teaching within a global context, interpreting it as an example of the way in which, using education as a covert instrument of 'neo-colonialism' (Macedo, 1994, p. xv), the wealthy 'First' World imposes its value-systems upon the impoverished 'Third' World. Freire's account of how 'pedagogy' can be used to colonize and control in this way might have been written specifically to describe the confrontation between Caliban and Miranda:

> Pedagogy which begins with the egoistic interests of the oppressors (an egoism cloaked in the false generosity of paternalism) and makes of the oppressed the objects of its humanitarianism, itself maintains and embodies oppression. It is an instrument of dehumanization. (Freire, 1990, p. 39)

One of the reasons why Miranda feels self-righteously aggrieved with Caliban is because she went to some pains to teach him language – only to have what she perceives to be her benevolence repaid with treachery. Freire and his followers would not even allow her the satisfaction of this degree of moral superiority. Donaldo Macedo, for example, argues that, far from initiating the poor into the full benefits of education, the rich teach them just enough to make their servitude more effective. Caliban, Macedo might suggest, presents a typical example of someone who has been taught nothing more than an 'instrumentalist literacy in the form of a competency-based skill banking approach' (Macedo, 1994, p. xv). In other words, Caliban has learnt enough language to respond to commands but not enough – as Freire would put it – to 'read the world' of oppression which has transformed him from being 'mine own King' into an 'Abhorred slave'.

We can imagine the sleight-of-hand which was worked in order to fob Caliban off with the 'word' while leaving Miranda and her father firmly in control of 'the world'. Say, for argument's sake, that shortly after their arrival on the island, the two newcomers feel an overwhelming desire for the taste of fresh meat. They ask Caliban to 'instruct' them – as he was later to offer to instruct Stephano – in the skills of marmoset-snaring. Spontaneous, non-judgemental, Caliban immediately complies. Why should he even think of keeping the information secret? His visitors are hungry and there are marmosets in plenty to share. He starts to tell them – haltingly, perhaps, for their language is new to him – how to construct a snare. 'Well', he might say, 'you take one of those . . . er . . . creeper thingies and you . . . er, kind of, er . . . twist it round a piece of wood sort of thing'. And so on. Miranda listens carefully. Perhaps she takes notes, for she is fluent in the written as well as the spoken form of her language. Later on, in private, father and daughter study their notes together. They decide to make a permanent, carefully structured record of the procedures which Caliban has taught them. Carrying the information in one's head is all very well; but memory can be unreliable – and what if one of them were to die? The knowledge might be lost forever. A written record would carry unassailable authority. It could also be copied, distributed around the world (for profit, perhaps) and passed down to future generations.

The act of transposing the information about marmoset-snaring from the spoken into the written word changes the nature of that information significantly. As long as Caliban is physically present to explain how it is done, Miranda can seek clarification by asking him to repeat certain points or by questioning him further on finer details. Caliban is able to support his sometimes vague and imprecise use of language with physical gestures. If the information about marmoset-snaring is only available through the medium of the written word, however, there is no room for ambiguity or imprecision. A clear sequence of instructions must be established. Phrases like 'creeper thingies' will not do. Detailed information is needed: what kind of creeper? What length is required? How thick should it be? Should the creeper be cut in the morning, afternoon, early evening, rainy season, once every three years? Precise names for each of the working parts of the marmoset snare are essential in case future snare-makers, who have not had the benefit of seeing Caliban's original device, get things wrong. And so, a whole new way of talking – a 'discourse' about marmoset snares – is established. Soon, it becomes impossible to be taken seriously as a marmoset-snarer unless one is fully conversant with the conventions of this discourse.

Once a correct procedure for marmoset-snaring has been established and codified in this way, it becomes necessary to think about ways of ensuring that 'quality control' is maintained wherever marmoset snares are to be set. How can we make sure that all our marmoset-snarers are operating to the same standard of efficiency? The answer is to establish a form of assessment. Aspiring marmoset-snarers can take an examination in their chosen trade. Those who pass the examination will receive a certificate declaring them fit to practise marmoset-snaring around the world. Those who fail the examination will not be allowed to practise – and if they attempt to do so, they will be punished.

What will the marmoset-snaring examination consist of? To be fully satisfied about would-be snarers' competence, the examiners might wish to assess them across the whole range of educational objectives described in Bloom's *Taxonomy* (discussed in my previous chapter). Each of Bloom's six areas might require its own mode of examination. A snarer's factual knowledge could be assessed through a series of multiple choice questions, where the candidate is presented with a choice of statements about the chosen subject and must decide which one is correct. An example might look like this:

The most effective wood for making a marmoset snare is:

a) oak
b) beech
c) willow
d) ash

Tick the correct answer.

Moving to the other end of Bloom's spectrum, 'evaluative' skills require a different medium of assessment, because they imply an ability to weigh up arguments, support assertions with evidence, and draw conclusions which may be most effectively addressed, perhaps, in a critical essay: 'The "Miranda" marmoset snare outstrips the "Caliban" prototype in design, technology and flexibility.' To what extent would you agree with this statement?

We could look at each of Bloom's six areas in this way, thinking about the skills implicit in each one and about the most effective means by which they might be assessed. Having created our assessment framework, we might be struck by the number and variety of skills we feel need to be demonstrated before a qualification in marmoset-snaring can be awarded with confidence. We may decide that there is actually a 'skills hierarchy' implicit in marmoset-snaring and that would-be snarers need to work their way up through a series of levels before they can be awarded their certificate. Perhaps only a select few will attain the highest levels and be allowed to become full practitioners. Those who cannot leap the ultimate examination hurdle will be relegated to more menial tasks such as gathering wood for the snares or cutting the creepers to size.

Where does all this leave Caliban, the inventor of the marmoset snare? Could he proceed through the examination levels and achieve his qualification? To do so, he would have to acquire a whole range of skills which are at present alien to him. More than this, he would have to exchange his whole identity and his beliefs for those of Miranda. Maybe he has the resolution and desire to do this. More likely, he will stare in bewilderment at the army of examiners, teachers, students and workers of varying status or degree which has closed ranks around the learning he shared so thoughtlessly. As he does so, he may scratch his head and wonder how he ever came to be 'written out' – literally – from 'the world' he thought was his.

Let us end this chapter where we began it – with Li, poised to share her discovery of the shrimping-net. If she could look into the future and see the fate that Shakespeare envisaged for Caliban (whom she resembles in so many ways) would she be so eager to return to her mother and her tribe? As soon as she makes the decision to pass on her learning, she will, as all teachers do, 'violate expectancy'. Her own expectancy will be violated in its turn. Whether the violation brings good or ill depends on how Li and the rest of her tribe answer these questions:

Where did this learning come from?
Why should it be valued?
Why should it be passed on?
How will it be taught?
Who will own it?
Who will benefit from it?
How will they gain access to it?
What will the consequences be?

The fate of every creature on the planet depends on the answers.

Response to 'Who Teaches and Why?'

Ian Davies

The three areas (teaching, assessment and alternatives) highlighted in Nick McGuinn's chapter encompass a huge number of issues. The complexities within each area are felt intensely by all professional educators. When they are taken together the problems may seem almost overwhelming. It is not easy to see clearly if McGuinn does more than raise issues for our consideration as opposed to developing a fully formed argument. Nevertheless there are suggestions within his piece of a particular view or, at least, preferences. These preferences are given at times in a reasonably direct way and occasionally can be implied from the sort of references and the style of argument that are made. I feel that the following points would provide some sort of guide to reading Nick McGuinn's chapter:

- Education can occur when people have been afforded the space and leisure to learn.
- Among the various possible types of teacher those who are determined to be egalitarian are to be most positively regarded.
- Gardner's ideas about multiple intelligences provide a useful way forward for establishing educational targets and processes.
- Experiential learning is preferred.
- Assessment is potentially very problematic.
- Alternatives need to be considered.

I would not want to disagree fundamentally with any of the above statements. And yet, it is important to examine each of these areas in turn if the nuances of Nick McGuinn's arguments are to be explored and if the potential disadvantages of what he suggests are to be realized.

Education Should Take Place in the Context of Leisure

In one sense few would want to disagree with Nick McGuinn's general position. If any task is to be completed in a thoughtful and useful manner then time and space needs to be allowed. Virginia Woolf (1984 edition) wrote of her need for a 'room of one's own'. Maslow in his famous 'Hierarchy' made it clear that basic needs must be met before higher order thinking and action can take place. Nick Tate when chief executive of the Qualifications and Curriculum Authority (the government agency that has an overview of much of the educational provision in England) made a number of high profile statements in which he argued that the best way to ensure the development of a tolerant society would be to ensure that people feel secure (Tate, 1995). In other words, they need to feel safe and to have the time and space in which to become educated. Various examples could be given to show some benefits of this approach. Code breakers during World War Two at Bletchley worked as a cloistered elite (Jenkins, 1991). Hermann Hesse's fictional representation of the highly educated saw them, away from the world, engaged in the 'glass bead game' (Hesse, 1979). Nick McGuinn suggests that people need to be 'granted the freedom to withdraw from the grind of daily life so that they can focus all their energies upon their studies'. All of this seems straightforward and obvious.

However, there are a number of arguments and illustrations that may lead us to resist, or at least question, this rather cosy view of the practice of education. It would be unwise to overstate matters. Nick McGuinn is not suggesting total isolation from the world. Much of his chapter is given over to the ways in which education can be developed in the world. And yet, given the way his chapter begins there are three points that do need to be made. First, there may be psychological issues about the way in which learning takes place. Cobb (1999) discusses a key debate in which 'constructivists analyse thought in terms of conceptual processes located in the individual; sociocultural theorists take the individual-in-action as their unit of analysis' (p. 137). Cobb concludes that 'learning is a process of both self-organisation and a process of enculturation that occurs while participating in cultural practices, frequently while interacting with others' (p. 145). In other words, if one were to 'withdraw from the grind of daily life' as Nick McGuinn writes, then learning would, in certain circumstances, be more rather than less difficult. Secondly, educators such as Midwinter (1972) have argued that societal considerations are important. This is not so much about Callaghan's point (as mentioned in Nick McGuinn's chapter) that society having invested will want to express a view as to how education is organized. Rather, it is a matter of judging the extent to which removal from the world is useful. Midwinter developed his arguments in relation to students in economically disadvantaged areas. He challenged the view that the existing local culture would be inadequate and that people needed to have their horizons broadened. He suggested (and in this he seemed to follow the work of people like Freire) that meaning had to be seen in the learners' immediate context. Only in this way he argued would it be possible for disadvantage to be understood and ultimately overcome. It is interesting that McGuinn relates his arguments to alternatives in education and refers in particular to the work of Freire. As such it is important to raise a third problem about the extent to which education is best organized away from the daily grind. It is important to consider Nick McGuinn's claim that he favours an egalitarian approach to learning. This area has social and political connotations that are highly significant.

Promoting the Egalitarian Teacher

Nick McGuinn's outline of the broad types of teacher is a useful starting-point. He makes it clear that there are various figures who should not be regarded as good role models. Lawrence's 'burnt out' idealist is not someone who attracts much more than our sympathy. Lawrence's experiences of education in Nottinghamshire and his fictional accounts in novels such as *Women in Love* are engrossing but appalling. Similarly those teachers who attach conditions to the learning process so that only limited outcomes are accepted are clearly not doing a good job. When a relationship is forged owing more to imperialism than dialogue, it is not attractive. Nick McGuinn's arguments for us to see intelligence in a variety of ways (following Gardner's ideas) are a useful and powerful recognition of the value of diversity.

But, again, there are tensions within the arguments in Nick McGuinn's chapter that need to be examined. Egalitarianism is an attractive word but it becomes merely a slogan if there is little elaboration of its meaning. The boundaries of acceptable goals and actions in an egalitarian society are never really made clear. In these circumstances we are forced to examine the way in which the chapter is written as well as the nature of the arguments. We may be reassured by the inclusion of a variety of very down to earth examples as well as illustrations from 'high' culture. On the other hand we may note that the nine quotations from Shakespeare and a series of references to Blake, Eliot, Lawrence, Raine and others do not seem immediately egalitarian. It would be unwise to descend into the sort of absurdities revealed by Robert Hughes (1993) in his blasts against political correctness in American universities. We really do not need to wonder if the telephone directory has more literary value than a play written by Shakespeare. We already know that the latter is richer and more worthwhile. And yet, given the nature of his arguments and his illustrations we may wonder about the meaning of Nick McGuinn's arguments. Where would he see himself in relation to the debates and challenges thrown down by Bloom (1987) (the well-known literary critic celebrated by his friend and Nobel prize-winning novelist Saul Bellow (2001) as *Ravelstein*) who argued that students' minds had been closed by attempts at egalitarianism?

Do Howard Gardner's Multiple Intelligences Add Up?

Nick McGuinn devotes a good deal of space in his chapter to an account of Gardner's theory of multiple intelligences. It seems in the way he discusses the intelligence of Caliban and the actions of Miranda that he sees multiple intelligences as a way of promoting the egalitarianism that is discussed. When we questioned above the meaning of Nick McGuinn's egalitarianism it seems that his reply would be an acceptance of, and a willingness to develop, a variety of intelligences in a process that is open and fair. The willingness to base these arguments around the work of Howard Gardner is understandable. Gardner's work has been enormously influential. The heading above is taken from a publication by John White (2000) in which the amazing impact of Gardner's ideas is described. A school in Australia has prominently displayed the message 'How many of your intelligences have you used today?' Thousands of so-called multiple intelligence (MI) schools have been opened in Australia and North America and the influence of this theory has been dramatic in schools in the UK. The theory is enormously attractive. For those who see the obvious (i.e. that people have different talents) it is both unfair and economically wasteful for only one sort of ability to be recognized. The existence of two cultures in our society (Snow, 1959) has been harmful. Why is there such a clear academic and vocational divide in schools? Why is it not possible to reward more equally the skills of the craftsperson, the academic and the entrepreneur? Indeed, is it not possible to go further and see the links between these different abilities? For example, it is possible to regard something like English literature as a narrowly academic subject suitable for those who are capable of intellectual thought and expression. But it is also possible to go further. English is, of course, also a focused vocational pursuit both in which specific job-related skills are developed and in which cultural capital is passed on to those who are being prepared for certain positions. Old-fashioned and discredited IQ (intelligence quotient) tests in which a so-called accurate measure of a person's overarching intelligence could be given in a culture-free context by the award of a simple number seems intellectually shoddy. IQ tests are also economically wasteful (as so many people are seen as failures) and politically unacceptable as scarce goods are made available only to the elite. To open up these issues can only be a good thing. The driving force behind Nick McGuinn's argument is very positive and to be welcomed.

However, general good intentions coupled with widespread impact are ultimately insufficient. It is necessary to question whether Gardner's ideas are coherent. White (2000) makes a devastating critique of the work of Gardner. He argues that:

> The seven or eight categories are too close to familiar curricular areas for comfort. They make curriculum planning deceptively easy. They tempt us to bypass the complex ethical and practical problems found in constructing a defensible curriculum in favour of a categorisation backed by all the authority of a Harvard professor. We may escape the shackles of IQ intelligence only to find ourselves imprisoned within another dubious theory (p. 35).

There is not enough space in this brief response to outline all the arguments that could be developed from White's conclusion shown above. However, perhaps one or two examples should be given. First, why are the particular seven or eight intelligences (the numbers vary depending on which publication one reads) included? White asks 'Why is linguistic intelligence in but the ability to recognise faces out?' (p. 6). Second, what can be done to consider the development of intelligences: are they fixed or without limit? Many more questions could be asked about Gardner's work.

What is the Nature of Experiential Learning?

Nick McGuinn makes a case for developing multiple intelligences by means of an experiential approach to learning. Again, he is able to draw on the work of many key educators. Dewey would not be unhappy with much of what he suggests. Nick McGuinn's references to Vygotsky show that his approach would not be haphazard. There would be a targeted system that would allow teachers and learners to collaborate in the development of progress. As such it is necessary only to raise a number of issues that seem not to have been fully explained.

I am a little unsure as to the overarching purpose of the education that is proposed by Nick McGuinn. It may be that something more refined than making a decision to emphasize either cognitive or utilitarian or 'progressive' goals (Ross, 2000) has been considered already but the nature of the preference has not been made very clear. Further, when considering teaching goals and procedures we are a little unsure as to the direction that would be established. In very general terms I would wish (following Evans *et al.*, 1996, p. 3) to suggest four rules for classroom action in relation to experiential learning:

- Depth of understanding is more important than coverage and superficial exposure.
- Topics and issues need to be connected through some kind of thematic, interdisciplinary or historical structure. Simply studying one issue after another will not be enough.
- The study of issues must be based in challenging and relevant content.
- Students must experience some measure of control, or at least significant involvement, in the teaching process.

Nick McGuinn may agree with the above (it would be unrealistic for us to expect him to have made clear all teaching strategies in the space of a short chapter). However, I am not entirely sure if he would agree and in any case I would need to know much more about what he would mean by such terribly indeterminate words as 'depth', 'challenging' and 'control'.

The Challenges of Assessment

Nick McGuinn rightly draws attention to the difficulties of assessing students' understanding and skills. He goes to some length to paint a picture which is in many ways a nightmare scenario of a competence-based assessment system, and which, unfortunately, seems to bear a good deal of resemblance to some of the practices that we currently accept. However, while we would agree with Nick McGuinn that these negative features must be omitted, or at least modified as best as possible, we need to know what, precisely, he is suggesting. It is possible to read his account which suggests that a learner will be '"written out" – literally – from the "world" he thought was his', as meaning that assessment should be avoided. Alternatively, he may mean that we simply have to think about the meaning that a form of assessment may have. His series of questions at the end of the chapter suggest that it is this latter approach that he adopts. Indeed, to suggest that assessment can be avoided entirely seems not only hugely unrealistic in the contemporary political and educational climate but also rather meaningless as we are constantly assessing or at least evaluating others throughout all our interactions. I suggest that we should not pretend that we can avoid assessment but rather that we need to consider the form that it should take. That Nick McGuinn does no more than entertainingly and intelligently tell us of the possible pitfalls of traditional systems is not enough.

The area of assessment is too complex for simple solutions to be proposed and fully elaborated here. Nevertheless we would argue for a beginning to be made towards a more meaningful and just assessment system by focusing on what could be called 'active procedural concepts'. Procedural concepts have been used for some time in history education (Lee and Ashby, 2000). Examples from that subject would include evidence, change and causation as opposed to substantive concepts such as revolution. Whereas substantive concepts might lead to the exploration of particular events (such as the French Revolution) procedural concepts would be more wide ranging. This would mean that learners had the opportunity to think as historians as opposed to thinking about history. Of course, the tensions between difficult matters such as the extent to which skills have to be practically demonstrated need a good deal more work. But focusing on procedural concepts would allow for discussions to take place about the essential purpose of a topic or theme. It would mean that assessment would be built into the programme. It would also mean that there would be links established between teaching and learning as learners were encouraged to explore and to demonstrate more complex understandings and action. It would go some way towards grasping the nettle of assessment rather than presenting it as inherently incapable of provisional resolution.

What is an Alternative?

Nick McGuinn's chapter warns us of the need to explore alternatives and not necessarily to accept the prevailing orthodoxy. I would concur wholeheartedly with this sentiment. However, I am unsure as to his meaning of 'alternative'. This is more than a semantic issue. I feel a little confused as to the nature of what can be explored and in what way. He demands that 'one must possess the courage to face the truth, no matter how unpalatable it might be'. Nick McGuinn, as has been said above, clearly feels (and rightly so) that Shakespeare is better than other authors. We also know that he dislikes certain versions of the truth. He seems, for example, to suggest that the opening lines of St John's Gospel give an unnecessarily restrictive view of the nature of the world. However, he also insists that 'The fundamental task of the teacher is to challenge complacency, to shatter preconceptions . . ..' We need to ask a number of obvious questions. Is it intended that teachers present Shakespeare as a great author in the process of introducing learners to the truth? Or is it proposed to allow for an exploration of language which, if it is successful in challenging complacency, will allow students to conclude that our most highly regarded authors are really not that good? He cannot have it both ways.

Conclusion

Nick McGuinn encourages teachers to be just, to explore alternatives and to be wary of simplistic assessment formulations. He encourages us to consider how and why people learn and how they can be taught. This is enormously valuable. There is a pleasing validity about his chapter in which he refuses to impose simple solutions. If he had made a series of recommendations it is unlikely that he would have been able in the short space available to convince all readers. His message of the need for careful and wide-ranging thought and appropriate action is carried through the medium of his carefully written chapter in which the reader has to think hard and seriously about important issues. This is the stance of a professional educator. The real test of his chapter will be if we are all (including the authors of this book) prepared to develop, at some point, clear expressions of our key ideas and recommendations for what should be done.

Activities

In Chapter 3, I consider what can happen to learning when it passes, through the medium of the teacher, into the social and political arena. I suggest that society has very high expectations of its teaching force and that teachers can use their powers for good or ill. Finally, I try to show how, by privileging certain kinds of learning over others, it is possible, literally, to 'write' the powerless out of education. The issues raised in this chapter are played out through the experiences of Shakespeare's Caliban. I focus upon this figure because I want to show how seemingly abstract ideas can have serious – and even tragic – consequences for individual human beings. Ian Davies is concerned that this dwelling upon a particular individual's experi-ence (even if we argue that Caliban represents all those who, in Freire's words, are condemned by the powerful to a 'culture of silence') might be a distraction from the real business in hand – the attempt to make 'recommendations for what should be done'. We resume this argument about the tensions between the personal voice and the needs of the community in Chapter 5.

As in Chapter 2, I have set out below a series of key questions designed to help you focus upon the key issues raised here by Ian Davies and myself. The questions are accompanied by a number of assertions (marked out as bullet points) to help you structure your response.

Key Questions

What is the purpose of a place of learning?
A place of learning should:

- provide a haven from the world in which individuals have the 'leisure' to pursue the knowledge which is important to them
- offer a model of what society might be, rather than reflect what it actually is
- engage with the communities which surround and sustain it by meeting whatever requests those communities make – be they cultural, spiritual, ideological, intellectual or economic
- offer open access to all who wish to use it, whenever they wish to use it, in the ways that suit them best
- grant access only to those deemed most likely to benefit from the experience.

What is the purpose of teaching?
The purpose of teaching is to:

- ensure continuity by passing on to the next generation the knowledge which is deemed most valuable by a society
- ensure stability by inducting the next generation in the norms, values and practices of a society
- prepare the next generation as adequately as possible to meet the unknown challenges which the future holds
- challenge human beings individually and collectively to look at the world with fresh eyes by 'violating' their 'expectancy'
- meet whatever learning needs individuals might have, whenever and however they declare them
- ensure that those who are deemed to have most to offer society receive the best access to knowledge.

What is the purpose of assessment?
The purpose of assessment is to:

- help learners consolidate and develop their learning
- help teachers identify and meet the learning needs of their students
- help a society to identify national and local learning needs and to allocate resources accordingly
- help a society decide who is most suitable to undertake the various roles and responsibilities essential to its survival

- ration access to limited educational resources so that those deemed most deserving gain most access
- affirm the learning deemed most valuable by a society
- determine what should be taught and how
- provide appropriate structures for helping teachers and learners reflect upon whatever is taught and learnt, however it is taught and learnt.

Suggestions for Reading

Cox, B. (1991) *Cox on Cox: An English Curriculum for the 1990s.* London: Hodder & Stoughton.

Cox, B. (1995) *The Battle for the National Curriculum.* London: Hodder & Stoughton. In 1988, Brian Cox was invited by the then Secretary of State for Education and Science in England and Wales to chair a Working Group to prepare proposals for English in the National Curriculum. These two texts provide an insider's account of the struggles which ensued. Although focused upon the particular example of English, Cox's accounts raise many general issues about the ways in which learning is valued and organized. The points he makes can be applied across the curriculum.

Freire, P. (1990) *Pedagogy of the Oppressed.* New York: Continuum.

Freire, P. and Macedo, D. (1987) *Literacy: Reading the Word and the World.* South Hadley, M.A.: Bergin & Garvey. Freire shows how education can be used by the powerful to dominate the weak and impose upon them a 'culture of silence'. He advocates a radical pedagogy which, by encouraging the powerless to channel their sense of alienation through the medium of collective action, can help them to challenge the forces of oppression and take direct control of their own lives. My description of the encounter between Caliban, Prospero and Miranda in Chapter 3 could be read in the context of Freire's work.

Raffan, J. and Ruthven, K. (2000) Monitoring, Assessment, Recording, Reporting and Accountability. In J. Beck and M. Earl (eds) *Key Issues in Secondary Education* (pp. 23–35). This chapter offers a brief and accessible guide to the key terms mentioned in the title. It considers the relationship between teaching and assessment and it offers explanations of such concepts as 'validity' and 'reliability'. The bibliography to this chapter provides a useful starting-point for further study.

Slavin, R. E. (1991) *Educational Psychology: Theory into Practice.* Boston and London: Allyn & Bacon. Chapter 14 offers a clear and practical guide to key assessment issues, explaining such terms as 'formative' and 'summative' assessment and 'norm' and 'criterion' referencing. Slavin also gives examples of different assessment strategies – such as multiple choice questioning. He discusses the rationale for these strategies and locates them within a theoretical context.

Tweddle, S. (1995) A Curriculum for the Future: A Curriculum Built for Change. *English in Education*, 29 (2): 3–11. Sally Tweddle tries to imagine the kind of English curriculum which might best meet the needs of people growing up in the opening decades of the twenty-first century. Her ideas make an interesting comparison with Cox's work. Particularly important for the purposes of this chapter, however, is the communicative framework Tweddle constructs in order to demonstrate how information is mediated and received within a social context.

Suggested Practical Activities

1. Think of an educational institution you have attended in the past or the one you are attending now. What values did/does that institution claim to promote? How successfully did/does it live up to its claims? What evidence do you have for making your judgement? To what extent has this institution helped you to develop as a learner? Do you feel loyalty and affection towards it? Compare your findings with those of a colleague who attended a similar institution – if you can find someone who did so in a different country, so much the better. As an extension activity, interview a teacher who worked/works in the institution and compare your experiences.

2. Think of an organization which you have attended and which is not directly associated with formal, classroom-based education. It could be a school or college society, for example, or some kind of community-based club or association. Using the focus questions outlined in the paragraph above, compare your experiences of this organization with your experiences of your chosen educational institution.

3. Can you think of an occasion when a classroom teacher successfully identified your 'zone of proximal development' and helped you to make some kind of breakthrough in your learning? Describe what happened. Think about the reasons why this act of teaching was so successful. Was it due to the teacher's personality? their chosen teaching style? the learning environment? your motivation? Now think of an occasion where the opposite occurred and ask the same questions.

4. Think of instances of successful and unsuccessful teaching which you have experienced outside the classroom. What similarities or differences between these experiences and those described in the previous paragraph do you notice? What conclusions do you draw from this?

5. Select two people to interview. One of them should be a person whose educational experience proceeded without interruption from nursery school to university. The other should be a person who either dropped out of the formal educational system completely or has returned to it later in life. Compare their experiences.

6. Interview someone who is interested in alternatives to the conventional educational system. It might be, for example, someone who educates their children at home or subscribes to Freire's principles of 'liberatory education' or is a supporter of the Steiner School system. Explore with them the reasons for their choices.

7. Think of an assessment process you have experienced at school or college. Looking back, what do you think its purpose was? Were you aware of this purpose at the time or have your thoughts about it changed? Did the assessment process allow you to show what you could do? Has the time and effort you put into preparing for the assessment proved to be of lasting value, or was it a temporary means to a particular end? If you were responsible for setting up this particular assessment process, would you change its structure and purpose in any way? If possible, interview someone who has that task now and tell them what it is like to be 'on the receiving end'. Ask this assessor for their views about the rationale behind, and the efficacy of, the chosen assessment system.

8. Think of an assessment process which you have experienced outside the classroom. Perhaps you took private music lessons, auditioned for a place in a band or participated in a sporting competition. Ask the same questions of this procedure as you did of your school or college experience. Compare the results.

9. Think of an area in which you have some expertise – making an omelette, playing guitar, swimming or whatever. Using the suggested background reading on assessment and my description of Caliban's 'marmoset-snaring' to guide you, construct a valid, reliable and appropriate assessment procedure for your chosen subject which would allow the person taking it to progress from 'Beginner' level. Invite a friend to try it out. What issues emerge? Can you successfully defend your assessment procedure?

CHAPTER **4**

Policy, Practice and Principles

Ian Gregory

Following on from the discussion in Chapter 1 let us accept that the concern for education is only intelligible against a background – a *conceptual* background – of notions like knowledge, ignorance, truth falsity, correctness, error, understanding. The task of education is to advance the cause of knowledge and truth, to help individuals to be correct rather than not, to allow individuals to understand better than otherwise they would. Let us further accept that in saying this we do not need to commit ourselves to any particular theory of truth. There is no need for our purposes to take a stand on whether critiques of traditional epistemology are justified. All that is required is that our epistemic notions – whatever their final status – enjoy currency in the society. It is, most of the time anyway, no part of radical critiques such as post-modernism to abolish these ways of talking. After all we will still need to make the distinctions high-lighted by our existing epistemic vocabulary no matter what the correct analysis of these notions. Something (for instance) very like the distinction presently marked out by knowing and merely believing a certain proposition is going to have to be drawn if our purposes and interests are going to be advanced. And so on across the entire range of distinctions drawn using our customary epistemic terms.

The importance of education lies in advancing knowledge, under-standing, the truth, and contrariwise in diminishing error, confusion and falsity. Its importance finds expression at the societal level in the huge efforts that are made at great cost by states to ensure their citizens enjoy an education. There is a shared conviction that young persons not having access to educational opportunities are greatly harmed. If the denial of such opportunities is deliberate and remediable our sense of *moral* outrage cannot be assuaged. If the lack of such opportunities is because a society simply does not have the resources to provide those opportunities and if it is within our society's power to go some way to affording educational opportunities to those so denied, political pressure mounts to try and aid that other country in making appropriate educational provision.

Educational provision always takes place within a given social, political and cultural context. Bearing this in mind let us consider the radical changes put into place in the education service of England and Wales over the last twenty years.

There can be no doubt that the changes of the last twenty years are radical. They go to the roots of the dispensation put in place by the great Education Act of 1944 (this will be referred to as the 44 Act). The changes of the eighties and nineties have transformed the relationships between those charged by legislation with responsibility for delivering the nation's schooling. Those changes in turn inevitably reflect the differing principles informing the thinking of those driving the agenda of change. To appreciate the extent of change and how and why it has come about we need to go back to the 44 Act and remind ourselves of its salient features.

The 44 Act

The 44 Act put into place what the courts came to call the 'Educational Partnership'. The redistribution of powers and responsibilities, rights and duties, between the constituent elements of the so-called educational partnership, brought about by recent education law gives us the measure of how radical are the changes brought about by the legislation of the eighties and nineties.

The notion of the educational partnership is best characterized in the words of Lord Diplock in the *Tameside* case (1976). 'The responsibility for carrying out the national policy for education is distributed by the Act [the Education Act 1944] between the Minister of Education [*now Secretary of State*] and *local education authorities*, acting in partnership, . . . and also *governors* . . . of the individual schools. . . . To these I add, and not as junior partners only, the *parents* of children of school age upon whom by section 36 is placed the primary duty of causing their children to receive efficient full time education suitable to their ages, abilities and aptitudes.'

Lord Diplock goes on to add immediately: 'Parental wishes as to the school to be attended by the child and what he is to be taught there are to prevail so far as is compatible with the provision of efficient instruction and training and the avoidance of unreasonable public expenditure.'

As is not unusual with many partnerships of whatever kind, one partner was overwhelmingly dominant. In the particular instance, the dominant partner was the local education authority (LEA). Central government in the person of the Minister and the Department of Education, Parents and Governing Bodies, were incidental to the day-to-day functioning of the education service and the life of schools in the maintained sector.

While by section 1 of the 44 Act the Minister was charged 'to promote the education of the people of England and Wales, and the progressive development of institutions devoted to that purpose, and to secure the effective execution by local authorities, under his control and direction, of the national policy for providing a varied and comprehensive educational service in every area', the climate of the time was hostile to, and indeed extremely fearful of, granting to central government an undue measure of control over the nation's education service. Until the 1980s the role of central government in the nation's education service was, in the main, limited to keeping an eye on things. Only rarely did central government make forays into the domain of policy – comprehensivization being the most striking example of its determination to effect change in the mid-1970s. It might make suggestions and, of course, local authorities would always bear in mind that government if so minded could always legislate to enforce its will but the day-to-day control of schools lay with local authorities in the guise of LEAs. The contrast with our present situation could scarcely be more stark.

The detail of the responsibilities enjoyed by LEAs under the 44 Act would take us too far from our essential story. But it has to be said that there was barely an area of the life of schools that LEAs did not crucially touch. Very importantly under Section 23 of the 1944 Act they had responsibility for what the Act called the *'secular instruction'* of the pupils. It is striking to note that the term 'curriculum' does not feature once in the 44 Act and that, indeed, the only reference to what shall be taught outside of religious education in schools was the one reference in Section 23 of the Act to secular instruction. And it was the very variability in curricular provision across the nation, the almost inevitable outcome of grounding responsibility for what was taught in our schools in individual LEAs, that occasioned some of the dissatisfaction leading eventually to the demand for a greater measure of central control over what was taught in the nation's schools.

LEAs were charged with planning school provision within their area. They had to ensure there were suitable and sufficient schools for pupils in the area for which they had responsibility in the light of the abilities and aptitudes of the pupils concerned (Section 8). This duty did not extend to being necessarily the provider, only to ensuring that such provision existed. LEAs were charged with providing all the services schools needed in order to deliver a satisfactory education to the children attending them. They had responsibility for things like providing transport to get children to school, school milk and meals, medical services such as dental care and hygiene, sight tests and the like, arranging for the cleaning of a person or clothing of any pupil found to be infested with vermin or some other foul condition, providing clothes and shoes for those pupils of parents who could not afford them.

They determined the budgets of those schools for which they had responsibility. They determined staffing limits. They decided how many pupils any given school would have. They appointed and fired staff. They employed inspectors and advisers to try to guarantee that a certain quality of education was being delivered in their schools. They could inspect schools as they saw fit. They determined the membership of the governing bodies of their schools. It was LEAs who made sure that parents were discharging their responsibilities to their children to attend school regularly or were delivering a quality of education meeting satisfactorily the child's educational needs in the event of having decided on home education. It was LEAs who oversaw the delivery of religious instruction in its schools and who ensured the wishes of parents in this area be respected and met. The foregoing list, partial and incomplete though it is, captures something of the overriding role of the LEA in the life of maintained schools under the 44 Act. The balance of power as between the constituent elements making up the educational partnership was overwhelmingly tilted in the direction of LEAs.

The story of the powers of governing bodies and parents, as the other constituent elements of the educational partnership, may be briefly told, disregarding complications in the story arising from the role of governing bodies in so-called *voluntary aided* schools. Every school had to have a governing body though there was no requirement that they had *to have their own governing body*. It was not unusual for a governing body to oversee the affairs of several schools at the same time. Anyone who was on a governing body prior to the 1986 legislation will willingly testify that the impact of governing bodies upon the lives of schools was minimal. Individual governors were little known to the school. The real powers of governing bodies were minimal. Wherever the decision-making centre was for schools it did not reside in a school's governing body. Essentially they existed to rubberstamp decisions taken elsewhere; meetings of governing bodies often turned into occasions of lending support to the head-teacher and the policy for the school initiated by the head. Their personnel were LEA appointees. Governing bodies were creatures of LEAs. In some ways they can be seen as emblematic of the measure of control LEAs enjoyed under the dispensation put in place by the 44 Act. Barely known to those who passed their daily professional lives in the schools, governing bodies were peripheral to the ongoing concerns of schools.

Under Section 36 of the 44 Act there fell to parents the responsi-bility to cause their children of compulsory school age to receive efficient full-time education suitable to their age, aptitudes and abilities. They could discharge this responsibility either by regular attendance at schools 'or otherwise'. In effect this meant (and means) that unless they make suitable arrangements for the edu-cation of a child outside the context of the school, the duty can only be discharged by ensuring regular attendance at school (Section 39 of 44 Act). Alternative arrangements to regular schooling most frequently take the form of 'home education'. The LEA has always been charged with superintending such arrangements and making sure a satisfactory educational provision is being made. (Section 37 of 44 Act). The responsibility to cause a child to receive efficient full-time education was encouraged by allowing parents to choose to send their child to an appropriate denominational school if so minded and, if it could be afforded, to buy an education for a child in the so-called private sector (the anomalously named 'public schools'). In keeping with the sensitivity to the religious sentiments of parents the right to withdraw children from the daily act of religious worship was ascribed parents as was a right of withdrawal from classes of religious education – the only *compulsory* element of the school curriculum embodied in the 44 Act. Section 76 laid down the *general principle* (promisingly one might think) that chil-dren were to be educated in accordance with parental wishes. The associated proviso governing the authorities' duty to educate in accordance with such wishes, and the decision of the courts in the case of *Watts v Kesteven County Council* (1955), soon made it clear that parental wishes were easily able to be disregarded by LEAs as they pursued the larger planning function imposed upon them by the 44 legislation. The general principle was subject to the proviso that such education should be compatible with efficient instruction and training and that it should not cause unreasonable public expenditure. The very wording of the proviso and the unambiguous tone of judicial utterance in the *Watts* case gave LEAs an almost untrammelled power in overriding parental wishes in the case of wishes not driven by a distinctively religious commitment. The LEA was very much the final arbiter of whether the provisos were satisfied and the reality was that parents counted for very little in decisions on the education and schooling of their own children. And parental influence upon wider policy issues affecting education was non-existent.

The order put in place by the 44 Act remained untouched in its essentials for 30 years or so. There arose in the 1970s a widely shared sense that the nation's schools were failing the nation. Famously these concerns were articulated in James Callaghan's 'Ruskin Speech' of 1976. The logic of the Ruskin Speech was a radical agenda for change. It is as well just to remind ourselves briefly of the key themes of Callaghan's speech if only to recognize how the concerns addressed in subsequent legislation were prefigured in that speech.

An Agenda for Change

I mention in no very particular order the following themes as indicative of, and giving substance to, the anxieties abroad during the 1970s. Inevitably there were *anxieties about standards*. There was a great deal of contemporary debate about the failings of young British pupils as against (in particular) their German and Japanese peers in respect of mathematical and scientific attainment. Informing all the ongoing debate was an acute sense that the huge investment in public education was not resulting in *value for money*. The lack of adequate standards in pupil attainment was one such indication of a lack of adequate return on that investment. There was the lament that schools were *failing the requirements of the nation*. In particular we were producing young individuals who lacked the skills essential to an advanced economy crying out for literate, numerate, scientifically and technologically oriented and skilled workforce. All of this was in turn linked to a school culture hostile to the world of work, a culture contemptuous of the vocational. The lack of regard for the vocational as against the academic partly further reflected schooling's disregard of its larger responsibilities to the wider community. In this context arose a determination to bridge the academic/vocational divide. There was more than a hint that our education service too much celebrated the individual as against the collective and, importantly, informing the Ruskin Speech was a theme that has been the motif of almost all subsequent legislation and policy – an insistence that the closed world of education be opened up. It is possible to discern in Callaghan's words, and much other political comment of the time, a paramount insistence that the stranglehold of the 'educational establishment' be broken. 'The secret garden of the curriculum' was to be entered by the non-professionals and schools and teachers were to be made-more accountable. The Ruskin Speech is a particularly striking intimation to the effect that no longer were the politicians prepared to leave the issue of education to those whose job it is to deliver it. There needed to be public participation in a debate about the aims and purposes of an education service in an ostensibly democratic society. The irritation with, not to say resentment of, the LEAs and teaching profession finding expression in the Ruskin Speech and much comment of the time has resonated right down to the present time. This sense of grievance, justifiable or not, among those charged with delivering the education of the nation's young yoked to the resolution of Mrs Thatcher, the Conservative Prime Minister, during the course of her administrations to see through the deliverance of the nation from an ideology sapping the nation's energies and resolve produced an educational agenda for change unimaginable to anyone basking in the familiarities born of the 44 Act. It is to these changes I will now turn, paying particular attention to the great Education Reform Act 1988 (ERA).

Effecting Change

It is a profound error not to recognize the ideological nature of the changes brought about to the nation's education service during the 1980s. At one level, of course, education is irredeemably a domain of ideological difference. Education takes as its ultimate concerns the development and shaping of individuals. Ultimately, judgements as to the kinds of individuals we wish to see as the final end product of the educational process inevitably rest upon final judgements on the kind of society we wish to see. In no very vicious sense the debate about educational ends is ideological. In education, ideology 'goes the whole way down'. During the course of the eighties central government became increasingly self-confident in its beliefs as to the best way to transform the nation's schools in accordance with the ideology that so motivated the Thatcherite years – the overriding conviction that the operation of the free market would have as transforming an effect upon the delivery of a decent educational product as the operation of the free market has in every other area of significant human concern. As government sought to introduce the disciplines of the market into the world of schools, it necessarily embarked upon a substantial redistribution of the powers and responsibilities, rights and duties, between those constituent elements who make up the educational partnership. The apotheosis of this energetic effort is, of course, the 88 legislation – the so-called Education Reform Act. The 88 legislation represents the bringing to fruition of tendencies already well established by previous legislation. As importantly, it is the harbinger of all that has happened subsequently. It is to the mapping of this raft of legislative changes I now turn.

The first tentative moves affecting partners of the educational partnership are to be found in the 1980 Education Act. For our purposes it is only necessary to draw attention to the requirement that henceforth (with one or two exceptions that need not concern us) all schools are to have *their own governing body*. The phenomenon of one governing body having responsibility for more than one school was eliminated. The Taylor Committee Report (1977) on the governance of schools had made wide-ranging recommendations about where decision-making should lie within schools. It made radical proposals about the structure, composition and powers of school governing bodies and its recommendations were overwhelmingly, in the main, going to be endorsed by subsequent legislation. The 1980 Act acted in the spirit of the Committee's report when it accepted that *teachers* and *parents as of right* should enjoy representation on school governing bodies. In real terms, the powers of governing bodies were not significantly affected by this bit of legislation, but a marker had been put in place that parents were increasingly going to count. This was, emblematically, reinforced by the further requirement that in future when LEAs rejected parental wishes in the matter of which school they wished their child to attend, they now had to *justify* their decisions by the giving of reasons for the decision arrived at. Giving substance to this need was the setting up of appeals committees, under the auspices of LEAs, to which parents could appeal with a view to having the LEAs' decisions set aside. Over time, and almost exponentially in the most recent past, the appeals mechanism put in place by the 1980 Act has been a potent weapon in the hands of parents dissatisfied with LEA decisions in the matter of expressions of parental preference as to which school they wish their child to attend.

Given our concern with the larger picture, it is the 1986 Education (No. 2) Act to which attention should now be directed. There is a significant augmenting of the influence and rights of parents, governing bodies now start to play an altogether more significant role in the life of schools and LEAs, for the first time, glimpse the diminished role they will play in the future life of the schools.

LEAs lose their natural majority on school governing bodies. Parents were granted *parity of representation on governing bodies with LEA representatives*. Pursuing the recommendations of the Taylor Committee, it was laid down in law that the local community via the mechanism of *co-option* would be significantly represented on school governing bodies. The inspiration behind the requirement that each school have its own governing body was a clear expression of the belief that such governing bodies would be more engaged and interested in the affairs and wellbeing of *their* school than a governing body distant from the school by virtue of its shared allegiances with other schools for which it might have responsibility. The emphasis upon increased parental representation and community representation is an effort to enhance the commitment to the schools for which governing bodies had responsibility. The thought is that a governing body made up of individuals who have an immediate attachment and loyalty to the school for which they enjoy responsibility will concern themselves with the affairs and wellbeing of the school that much more seriously. Effectively for the first time, governing bodies are given both responsibility for *staffing* and *curricular concerns*. It falls to governing bodies to decide whether there will be sex education in their school, and if so what the content of sex education programmes will be. It falls to governing bodies to ensure the delivery of a suitably non-indoctrinatory mode of political education. They become responsible for the appointment of staff, below the level of deputy head and head. They become involved in matters to do with exclusions from school, staff discipline, and more generally discipline within schools. The 88 legislation adds to their responsibilities of governing bodies in all the areas mentioned.

The importance of the parent body is reinforced by the requirement that once a year there should be a *parents' annual meeting* at which an annual report should be made to parents by the governing bodies, headteachers and LEAs on how they are respectively discharging their responsibilities. And both the 80 and the 86 legislation significantly address the statutory entitlements of parents in the matters of information about the school which their children attend. More and more schools are forced by succeeding legislation to account to parents on both what the school does and achieves, and what its policies are in key areas of the conduct of school life.

The only partner to the educational partnership whose ostensible influence over the daily life of the school has not *yet* been changed is central government. But it is central government which is driving the agenda of change. The 80 and 86 legislation are only the opening shots in realizing that agenda of change. The Education Reform Act builds upon the changes already in place and gives the final and fullest expression to the government ambition of putting into place a version of a market-driven national education service. All the themes informing the 88 legislation are, however, already implicit in the previous legislation of the eighties: freeing schools from the distant bureaucracy of the LEA, the raising up of the parent as a key player in the education of our young, and giving a much greater measure of control over the life of individual schools to governing bodies. The Education Reform Act brings to a culmination all the foregoing legislative tendencies.

The Education Reform Act (ERA) 1988

It is difficult to overestimate the influence of ERA (often referred to below as the 88 Act). By any token it is an Act of immense significance in the history of education. It not only sets to nought so much of the 44 legislation, it is also highly unlikely that the main elements of the structure put in place by ERA will be dismantled by any future government of the foreseeable future. Politicians of all hues shared the opinion that the old regime could not deliver what was demanded of a modern schooling system. Crucial to this analysis was the sense that the bureaucracy of LEAs has been unresponsive to the needs and demands of the individual schools. Ways of dismantling this bureaucracy had to be found and the freeing of individual schools from the embrace of LEAs is perceived as an almost unproblematic good by all concerned – schools and politicians.

The market philosophy informing ERA, crudely expressed, amounted to the following: standards need to be driven up. The mechanism that will bring about the kind of pressure upon schools to drive up standards will be via expressions of parental choice. Parents are the clients of schools and what they have to offer. Good schools will thrive because they respond to parental demands. Bad schools will go to the wall unless in the face of parental demands they make more vigorous efforts to meet parental wishes and wants. What the legislation does is put in place mechanisms that make the reality of parent as client a major factor in the life of schools.

The 88 Act is a monumental piece of legislation. It is, however, possible to highlight those elements within it that put flesh upon the ambition to expose schools to the rigours of competition – competition being the key to the operation of any free market. If for nothing else ERA will be remembered for implementing a National Curriculum and a whole associated paraphernalia of attainment and assessment arrangements. The case for and against a National Curriculum is a complex matter. In terms of the encouragement of a market operative in the life of schools the *absolutely critical* point is not the rationale underlying the National Curriculum but rather, that as put into place and operationalized, it affords parents and the wider public a common currency in terms of which comparative judgements can be made as to how well individual children are doing as against other children, how well one school is doing as against another school, and how well one LEA's schools perform as against the schools of other LEAs. The paraphernalia of attainment targets, Key Stages 1, 2, 3 and 4, and nationally administered assessment tests for the nation's young, certainly encourages the belief that more reasoned and objective judgements can be made on how well the nation's schools are delivering against targets laid down for the schools. Over time it might be possible to make surer judgements about whether indeed standards are rising within the nation overall. All of these are matters for continuing debate. What cannot be gainsaid, however, is that it looks (perhaps illusorily) as though parents can now make choices on the basis of other than hearsay and gut reaction. In short, armed with the kind of information the National Curriculum provides fully in place, the exercise of parental choice is that much more significant because so much better informed. What now seems to be accepted on all sides is that parents are entitled to the very best information that is relevant to their child's education. The days, not so distant, when teachers could keep parents at arm's length have well and truly gone. Parent are here to stay as a voice to be heeded in the education of their children.

The role of parents as clients and consumers is further reinforced in other key respects – not so much independent of what has gone before but as part of a total offering to the parent body. Choice is enhanced if one has more choices. Government in the 88 legislation enlarged the scope of choice in the following ways: new categories of school were introduced; talk of City Technology Colleges (CTCs) and Grant Maintained Schools (GMS schools) entered educational parlance. Most important from our perspective are GMS schools. Their distinguishing feature was that their funding was directly from the Department for Education (DFE). On the back of a *parental ballot* all links with LEAs were sundered. Schools who 'opted out' became wholly free-standing, autonomous institutions who through their governing bodies became wholly responsible for the affairs of the school. Government saw the GMS school as being in the vanguard of its desire to encourage schools to compete so as to raise academic standards in the nation's schools. If all schools were in the market place competing with each other to attract parental expressions of preference because of what the school stood for, the benefits of the market place would be made manifest. Because they would be wholly autonomous, governing bodies would enjoy all the powers and responsibilities necessary for the government of such institutions. The LEAs would be nowhere to be seen. It can easily be seen that a nationwide system of GMS schools would have transformed the educational landscape. As events transpired, for the great generality of schools far more significant (and liberating) was the mechanism put in place in ERA of the local management of schools (LMS). And it is here that the inspiration of the market as the shaper of our educational system can be seen most starkly. The law surrounding LMS is very complex but in its essentials the story can quickly be told. LEAs by law are compelled to devolve down to individual governing bodies responsibility for managing their own school budgets. Governing bodies have to manage the school within the limits of their budgets. It falls to governing bodies to determine priorities, and allocate resources from their budget in the light of what their priorities are. A most striking example of the new freedoms that fall to governing bodies is that they decide upon staffing levels within a school. While constrained by the statutory requirement to deliver the National Curriculum, and meet the various other statutory curricular requirements laid down in law, governing bodies have the ability to use the money of the schools for those purposes that seem to them most helpful to the school at a given time. This overall responsibility in law for the budget of schools in the maintained sector gives to governing bodies a level of influence over the day-to-day life of schools never previously enjoyed.

What has so transformed the situation is that individual school budgets under the 88 Act largely reflect the ability of a school to attract pupils. The more successful a school is in attracting pupils the more money it has for governing bodies to expend as they so decide. The less successful a school is in attracting pupils the less money it has. The formula that controls the amount of money LEAs devolve down to the individual schools is largely pupil driven, according to the age range of the pupils, so each individual pupil attracts a certain amount of money. Translated into the individual budgets of the schools it makes a profound difference to the money any individual school has to deliver education for its students. Whereas previously LEAs could protect individual schools from, for whatever reason, their failure to attract their due quota of pupils, they no longer can. The financial wellbeing of schools is crucially bound up with their ability to persuade parents to send their children to them. The theme informing government policy is that successful schools will thrive, the unsuccessful, unless they turn themselves around, will go to the wall. Henceforward governing bodies simply could not be indifferent to pupil intake. They had to compete for parental allegiance.

Compounding all of these new realities is the government, giving more real substance to parents' rights in the matter of choice of their child's school. For the first time, the ability of a parent to express a preference about the school they wish their child to attend is buttressed in law in a manner that limits the ability of LEAs to deflect parental wishes. As we have seen, LEAs invoking the wide proviso of the 44 Act about 'the efficient use of resources' and the clear expression of the courts on the significance of the 'general principle' that children be educated in accordance with parental wishes, had treated expressions of parental wishes lightly. It was no longer going to be so easy. It is laid down in the 88 Act that the only grounds upon which an expression of parental preference can be set aside is if the school to which they wish to send their child cannot physically accommodate that child. At a time at which demographic trends mean that schools were awash with surplus places, the parental voice suddenly became altogether more important. Fairly clearly, the policy had within itself self-frustrating possibilities as successful schools found their very success allowed the invoking of the physical impossibility of accommodating any more children. Admission policies had to be put in place to regulate demand for places, and ironically schools found themselves in the position of choosing children on the basis of parents rather than, as was always envisaged, parents choosing the school. It is, perhaps, important to note that despite all the rhetoric parents *do not have the right to choose a school for their child*. What they do have, and have always had, is *the right to express a preference as to which school they wish their child to attend.* What is undeniably true is that the 88 Act for the first time gave more substance to the latter right. Along with much else, LEAs have lost the ability to set to one side easily such expressions of preference.

Some Concluding Remarks

Conceptualizing the changes of the last twenty years in terms of *winners* and *losers*, the LEAs are the great losers. Successive governments have removed their day-to-day influence over the life of schools. Central government has been the great winner, not only driving the agenda of change but also taking to itself a huge raft of powers designed to give it the overriding voice in the life of schools in particular, and the education service more generally. Governing bodies have been raised up as key players in the lives of the school for which they have responsibility – both at the strategic level and below. Parents are seen as crucial in the politics of education – both by central government in aiding them in creating a market and in making schools more accountable, and by individual schools as clients to be courted.

These substantial changes have been made within a society purporting to be liberal, democratic and pluralistic. Are the changes put in place and the principles seemingly informing them, changes and principles of a piece with the kind of society we claim to be?

I mention as cause for concern the following: the quite extraordinary measure of control over the nation's schooling enjoyed by central government; the unwarranted celebration of parental rights over children's rights in recent law and policy; the characteristic disregard of the professional voice as a key voice in the shaping of education policy. Let me elaborate a little.

It is a defining feature of a liberal outlook to insist upon the primacy of the individual. We might say the state exists to serve the individual rather than the individual to serve the state. Totalitarian regimes see the collective good as of overriding importance. This invariably goes with an attitude of mind that sees government as knowing what is best for people. Government takes it upon itself to promote a preferred way of life. The agencies of the state are directed to ensuring the acceptance of its favoured goals. In the pursuit of its ambitions, the independence of the education service is the first casualty. Schools promote the official ideology, universities encouraging independence of mind are closed down. In the ordinary course of events, liberals are deeply suspicious of the exercise of such *paternalism* (defined as taking decisions on another's behalf either because one knows what is best for them or to protect them from themselves). Suspicion of paternalism is compatible, nevertheless, with the state having an interest in advancing the interests of those citizens. Translated into the domain of education, the state can be concerned to secure their right to education. But, in keeping with liberal principles, securing the right to education does not *necessitate* the state entering into the educational arena in the manner characteristic of the last twenty years. John Stuart Mill, the great Victorian liberal theorist in his *On Liberty* (1859), gives expression to his deep suspicions about the role of the State in education. He feared a tyranny of the mind arising from granting to the state too much influence over the shaping of young minds. He would certainly have been horrified by the powers presently granted central government over the nation's education service. It is (perhaps) surprising that a liberal society has so readily acceded to an education service that is the most centralized in the contemporary world. Mill saw the state as limiting its concern to ensuring that the education on offer was of a satisfactory quality. He envisaged diverse providers of educational possibilities – thus avoiding the possibility of a prevailing intellectual and moral orthodoxy detrimental to the growth of individuality within society. The possibilities represented by the present dispensation and the very recessive role for the state countenanced by Mill are at the extreme ends of the spectrum. There are a whole host of possibilities between these extremes which respect the rightful interest of the state in the interest of its people and the potential of individuals to shape their lives as they see fit.

Compulsory education looks for its moral justification in the direction of providing children with the opportunities to develop their potentialities. Compulsory education is an exercise in paternalism in that young people have to attend school, enjoy some kind of education, whether they want to or not. Whether they know it or not, it is for their own good. The thought is that we are justified in limiting their freedom in the here and now so that, having been educated, they can exercise their freedom more significantly in the future. The children's rights movement often claims that vulnerable and immature as children might be, their independent rights to order and shape their own lives are too often denied. And nowhere more so than in education. One of the truly striking features of education law in England and Wales is the complete silence on the matter of children's rights. The education of the young, in all of its essentials, is exclusively a matter for the state and for the parents. The officially inspired disapproval of more child-centred pedagogies of recent years, the increasing emphasis upon defining success in education by how it measures up to government laid-down standards of attainment, has reinforced such tendencies. The apotheosis of this disregard of the child's voice is to be found in the areas of sex education and religious education. It is difficult to think of areas of human concern of more significance to the shaping of individual minds. In a liberal society, we would normally feel people have the right to make up their own minds where they stand of such fundamental issues. Under our law, parents have the final voice on whether their children should enjoy the benefits, or not, of these key areas of education. And bearing in mind that 'a child' is defined as anyone under the age of 18 years old, we can see how far the remit of the parents run. This must be deplored.

The status of parental rights in education is, however, deeply ambivalent. While they enjoy in law almost proprietorial control over the sex and religious education of their children, parents are not trusted to be the best judges of that curriculum content making up the National Curriculum. They have no say in the matter of the recurrent assessment of their children at the key stages. There needs to be serious debate about parental rights, their nature and scope. If education takes, in keeping with the inspiration of liberal philosophy, the wellbeing of the individual child as its primary concern, on what grounds is it imagined that parents must know what is best for their child? We need to think afresh issues associated with parental rights – their grounds and their scope. As we work out a principled accommodation between the interest of the state in the education of its young, parental rights and the rights of children, can we possibly be satisfied with the dangerous measure of control over our schools vested in central government?

I conclude by emphasizing a key presupposition that has informed government thinking of the last 25 years or so. The determination of politicians to have a greater voice in educational matters, indeed to seize control of the educational agenda, can be seen as an expression of the belief that 'education is too important to be left to teachers'. Beginning with Winston Churchill's determination not to thank teachers for their contribution to the war effort, the relationship between teachers and politicians has always been rather distant. It will not have escaped notice that teachers were never seen as constituent elements of the 'educational partnership' put in place by the 44 Act. All recent governments have seen teachers as part of the problem afflicting the nation's schooling. Whether that sentiment can be justified or not, there is an important sense in which within the context of a democracy it must be true that education is too important to be left to teachers. All of us as citizens have an interest in our education service. As citizens, we have a stake in the products of our nation's schooling, the kinds of individuals our schools promote, the impact of educational provision upon our society at large. As members of a democracy, our voice demands to be heard on educational matters. This is not to say, of course, that the professional voice should be disregarded. While teachers as teachers have no more insights into the proper aims of education than the rest of us, while they should not enjoy a privileged voice on such matters, it seems the merest good sense that government should not exclude them from the decision-making processes informing the shaping of policy in this fundamental area of human concern. Teacher morale in the form of a sense of professional self-esteem and worth must be central to the realization of educational ambitions. Without teachers committed to providing the very best education society deems desirable, all our hopes will come to nothing. Whether the welter of legislation of the nineties designed to bring further pressure to bear on teachers, schools and LEAs to improve (or else!) does anything for that commitment is a matter for debate.

The upshot of this very cursory set of observations about the interests of the different parties to the education of the young poses the hardest of problems for a liberal and democratic society. How do we do justice to all the rightful but competing claims in determining what the aims of our education system should be? It cannot be good for a liberal society that the tentacles of central government reach so far into our schools as they work to provide education for the young. We need to find ways to revitalize educational debate. Education is too important to be left to teachers. But, as importantly, it is too important to be given over to central government.

Response to 'Policy, Principles and Practice'

Nick McGuinn

I wonder what Peter Dickinson's heroine Li – whose breakthrough in conceptual understanding I took as the starting-point for my first chapter – would have made of the educational landscape described here by Ian Gregory? We could argue, after all, that her intellectual curiosity set in motion the momentous chain of events which led, in time, to the implementation of the 1988 Education Reform Act to which he attaches so much importance.

Would Li be pleased to see where her discovery has taken us? She might be glad to know, perhaps, that the state, our modern-day equivalent of her tribe, is committed to the idea of education for everyone up to (and now increasingly beyond) the age of 16. Li had to venture off alone and puzzle out her learning for herself. Today, however, having absorbed Vygotsky's concept of the 'zone of proximal development', we try to assist and accelerate young people's learning in every way we can. We gauge their potential and measure their progress by subjecting them to a battery of formative and summative assessment procedures. We place young learners within a secure environment dedicated to the pursuit of knowledge. We support their learning by providing them with professionally trained teachers and other experts who are, in their turn, supported by a rich variety of resource materials ranging from detailed curriculum documents to the latest computer technology.

Li would quickly realize that education is taken very seriously indeed in our twenty-first-century society. Why, then, does Ian Gregory end his chapter on a cautionary note? Although pleased that the state should provide the means by which education might flourish, he is concerned, like Althusser, lest it dictate what the content and purpose of that education might be.

Is Ian Gregory's concern justified? If government offers its people certain rights – the right to national security, for example, or the right to an education – it seems reasonable that the same government should be allowed to impose obligations in return. Just as citizens might expect to be called to arms in defence of their state if it were under threat, might they not also expect to be 'mobilized' in the cause of other social enterprises dedicated to the collective good – such as an educational initiative like the current National Literacy Strategy, perhaps?

Why should a democratic state not seek to transmit its ideology through education? If the plays of Shakespeare, for example, are not taught, compulsorily, as part of the syllabus for Standard Assessment Tests in English at age 14, how can we be sure that the cultural heritage he has bequeathed us will be passed on for future generations to enjoy? If a requirement to study The Holocaust is not written into the curriculum for History or Religious Studies, say, is there not a danger that those terrible events will be forgotten?

Ian Gregory himself argues that: 'the importance of education lies in advancing knowledge, understanding, the truth, and contrariwise in diminishing error, confusion and falsity'. Societies need to have a clear, shared understanding of what those abstract nouns might actually mean in practice. A pluralistic democracy might interpret them in terms, for example, of: equality under the law; respect for other people and tolerance of their beliefs; a rejection of violence and confrontation in favour of discussion and negotiation. As a democratic citizen, I can reasonably expect that the school I send my children to will uphold and promote those principles. I cannot sit in the classroom and monitor what takes place there myself, so I rely on the representatives of the state, whom I have elected through the ballot box, to monitor on my behalf the education my child is receiving. Should these representatives discover that a school and its teachers are undermining democratic principles – by teaching a racist curriculum, for example – I would expect them to take appropriate action.

By saying this, I am conceding the principle that there are occasions when I as a parent can expect the state to represent me and to take action, on my behalf, which will directly affect my child.

Viewed from the perspective of parents and children – who, in the current jargon, are sometimes described as 'consumers' of education – a concept like 'paternalism' might not seem as negative as Gregory suggests. We expect the state to protect vulnerable members of society, such as the sick or pensioners or the unemployed; why should we not also expect it to speak up on behalf of children? Teachers may resent government inspection as an implicit questioning of their professional autonomy; but for the child condemned to endure uninspired and poorly planned teaching in a school which, perhaps, pays scant attention to individual learning needs, an inspector's report could provide effective – even life-changing – pressure for change.

One could take this line of argument further by suggesting that all the major policy decisions regarding education which have been made in the wake of James Callaghan's 'Ruskin Speech' have been designed to place children's needs at the heart of the teaching and learning process. I am old enough to remember the world Callaghan complained about, because I began my teacher training in 1976, the year he made his speech.

What did I find when, as a student teacher, I entered what Callaghan and others called the 'secret garden' of education? I discovered that it was possible for pupils to pass their entire school career up to the age of 16 without taking a public examination. The adjective 'public' was not always entirely appropriate: teachers could, if they wished, create their own assessment procedures and mark their pupils' scripts themselves, so that the English examination I designed for my students in School X might look significantly different from the English examination a colleague might design for her students in School Y. I discovered, too, that individual education authorities – and even individual schools – exercised a major influence over the curriculum. Thus, while one set of Year 7 pupils might be following a timetable composed of discrete 'traditional' subjects like Maths, Science and History, their counterparts in another school down the road might have their learning addressed by means of a 'topic web', where teachers took a particular theme like 'the weather' or 'the seasons' and built in opportunities for work in science or English or maths through activities arising from the topic.

Here indeed was something resembling that world of 'diverse providers of educational possibilities' which, Ian Gregory tells us, the Victorian liberal theorist John Stuart Mill had envisioned as an ideal. For somebody new to the profession, as I was then, such freedom and authority were exhilarating. I liked the fact that my

professionalism was respected. Because I had studied English Literature at university, it was assumed I could teach it – to Scholarship
level if necessary. Certainly, my one-year teacher-training course had
equipped me with plenty of exciting ideas for encouraging what was
then known as 'personal growth': the process by which young people
explore the world around them, and their relationship to that world,
through the medium of language. But this sense of professional
freedom was disconcerting as well.

I had joined a department of gifted individuals. We might discuss
aspects of our work over coffee occasionally, but we rarely sat down
as a team to review our policy and practice, to collaborate on the
creation of schemes of work, or to plan our way forward. Professionally, I felt very much on my own. How could I be confident, for
example, that I was teaching my students what they needed to know
– as opposed to what I enjoyed? My classes read novels in plenty and
wrote lots of stories; but I wonder how often we studied non-fiction,
for example, or analysed the structures of written and spoken
language at word, sentence and whole-text level?

What did it feel like to be on the receiving-end of such teaching?
I recall meeting again in Year 10 a pupil whom I had taught when
she first joined the school in Year 7. We started reminiscing about
the 'good old days'. 'Do you remember', she said with a nostalgic
smile on her face, '"Harlequin Avenue"?' 'Harlequin Avenue?' I did
remember. We had devoted about a month's worth of lessons to it.
'Harlequin Avenue' was the name of an English 'topic web' I had
devised with this girl's class when she was in Year 7. The theme of
our work was a study of 'soap operas'. We created a fictional street
and filled it with fictional characters. We invented 'families', drew
and labelled pictures of houses, cut out photographs from magazines
to represent our protagonists, devised dramatic situations for them
and then wrote, taped and filmed the consequences. I had enjoyed
the work and, judging by the fact that one of the pupils could still
remember it so fondly three years later, I think they had too.

Looking back at 'Harlequin Avenue' 25 years later, I am not so
sure that it actually was the great teaching success I assumed it to be
at the time. My job now involves training others how to teach
English; and I have to admit that if one of my students presented me
today with a scheme of work similar to the one outlined above, I
would have some searching questions to ask about it. First, I would
want to know precisely which aspects of National Curriculum
English 'Harlequin Avenue' addressed. I would want to know what
opportunities it offered for work in the various 'strands' which are

'woven into' the English curriculum: drama, for example, or information and communications technology. I would want to know how 'Harlequin Avenue' consolidated and extended the pupils' previous learning. I would ask how the scheme of work was differentiated to accommodate individual pupils' learning needs and learning styles. Above all, I would want to know what the pupils were going to learn and how the teacher intended to prove that such learning had actually taken place.

This difference in attitude towards 'Harlequin Avenue' expressed by my younger and older selves sums up the dramatic changes in education which have occurred as a result of the 1988 Reform Act. A somewhat haphazard but creative spontaneity has given way to something more serious, rigorous and, perhaps, dull. In 1976, my main concern as a teacher was to find exciting and inspiring things for my pupils to do; today, the emphasis is upon the identification, attainment and evaluation of learning outcomes. My younger self would have said to the Year 7 pupils and their parents: 'Trust my professional judgement. "Harlequin Avenue" will inspire exciting and purposeful work in English.' My older self would ask the teacher on behalf of those children and parents: 'What will the pupils learn by doing this and how will you prove that they have learned it?'

Which teaching style would you prefer to encounter if you were still a school pupil? The enthusiasm of the young man or the rigour of his older counterpart? Whom would your parents prefer to have as your teacher? To opt for one or the other is to make a very definite choice about the nature and purpose of education. The young man I have described here is like a sower of seeds. To him, the process of education is something of a mystery: he scatters the seeds and they sink into the complex soil of the human personality. Some germinate and blossom – perhaps straight away, perhaps years later – some die without ever reaching the light. The older man is like a gardener. He selects his planting-ground with care, nurturing the seedlings with precisely calculated measures of food and water. Instead of blooming wildly and magnificently where they will, his plants are staked in neat rows. The time as well as the place of their harvesting is determined by the gardener.

Both educational approaches have advantages and disadvantages. For those students who are 'in tune' with the 'seed-sower', learning can be a magical, inspirational experience. But what about the ones who cannot respond to his invitation? It may be that their preferred learning style is incompatible with his, or that they do not possess enough of the basic technical skills to work at the pace he sets them.

Perhaps they have done so many 'topic webs' of this kind before that they cannot stomach the thought of yet another one. Maybe they feel that imaginative engagements with language – particularly in its narrative form – will not equip them for the linguistic needs of the world beyond the English classroom, let alone the school gates.

The 'gardener' would have confident answers for all those concerns. The strength of his educational approach is its focus upon assessment and accountability. Armed with reading ages, spelling scores, cognitive ability tests and standard assessment levels (measured at ages 7, 11 and 14) he can devise for each of his pupils elaborate individual educational plans which will help them to move logically and coherently through the curriculum from the age of 5 to the age of 16. This approach also has its disadvantages, however. The main problem is that it privileges linguistic intelligence over all other forms; and this problem is compounded by the fact that education is mediated and assessed through modes of spoken and written discourse which are not always familiar or accessible to students.

Even if this were not the case, assessment can, of its nature, be a double-edged sword. If you give me a maths test in order to identify my strengths and weaknesses and then act on that information to help advance my mathematical understanding, well and good. If, however, you give me a maths test because access to the highest levels of mathematical knowledge is so expensive it has to be rationed and you want to see who is most deserving of that access – then I am not so sure. We can take this issue further. Think about how it might feel to know that the average student for your age group is expected to attain a National Curriculum Maths Level 7 – and yet you are only capable of a Level 5. And how might it feel to be a pupil (or a teacher, for that matter) in a school where most of the students only achieve Level 5 or lower – while five miles away on the other side of town there is another school where most of the pupils are achieving Level 7 or higher? Perhaps this awareness of public 'failure' is just the incentive you need to try harder. You may, on the other hand, lose all motivation and, in a desperate attempt to protect your self-esteem, pretend that you never cared about maths anyway.

Sowers and gardeners; the Acts of 1944 and 1988 – there are no panaceas, no single right answers where education is concerned. Ian Gregory suggests that one way forward might be to listen more closely to the child's voice. If we took this challenge seriously and asked our pupils what they think of their education, we might be quite disturbed by the answers. Perhaps they would say, 'My school is an intellectual, aesthetic and spiritual treasure-house where, under the care of charismatic teachers, I learn what it means for a human being to be fully alive.' They might, however, answer very differently: 'My school is a shabby, factory-like building where harassed and over-worked teachers struggle to educate their pupils against the odds – odds created by poor facilities, overcrowded classrooms and, above all, a pupil culture which is anti-intellectual and intolerant of diversity or personal expression.' We could probe a bit further by asking how many of our pupils actually enjoy going to school – and I mean 'enjoy' in the sense that Li enjoyed and was totally engaged by the rapt creative experience of thinking her way from spider's web to shrimping-net. I suspect that the answer to this question would be disappointing.

The root of the problem – and this takes us back to the central argument of Ian Gregory's chapter – is that our education system is based upon force. Education is imposed by the powerful (adults) upon the weak (children). We take all our young people – each of whom is a complex mixture of different abilities, needs, personalities and learning styles – and we force them, by law, through what is in effect a 'one-size-fits-all' education system. Why do we do this? Is it because we want to foster in each child that spirit of intellectual curiosity and creativity which Li seemed to be born with? Is it because we are actually scared of the energy and rebelliousness of young people and think that, by putting them in school, we can 'keep them off the streets' and indoctrinate them into compliance with our ways and values? Is it because in our society everybody needs 'to know their place' and the education system is the means by which we decide who will be the computer programmers and who will be the street cleaners?

What would happen if we removed force from the educational equation? I suspect that there would be a mass exodus of adolescents from our classrooms, each one delighted at the thought that they would never have to study Shakespeare or Physics or French again. Those who remained at their desks would be the ones who loved learning for its own sake. They, too, would heave a sigh of relief. Imagine what it must feel like to be a shy but intellectually curious student whose chance of an education has been ruined by disruptive classmates. Imagine what it must feel like to be a teacher who is passionate about their subject but whose enthusiasm has been ground down by years of trying to convey that enthusiasm to pupils who neither know nor care about it. If our schools were cleared of all the 'conscripts', would they not at last become true centres of learning and enlightenment?

Maybe. But what would happen to the ones who declined the offer of education? Illiterate, innumerate, unaware of the world beyond their immediate neighbourhood, how long would it be before, like their early nineteenth-century predecessors, they became the slaves of the unscrupulous and the predatory? What kind of society could survive such a fierce division between its 'haves' and its 'have nots'?

So we return to our original dilemma. Do we say that, being adults and therefore knowing what is best for the young, we insist that they experience the educational system which we, in our wisdom, have devised for their benefit? Do we say, 'Education is here for you if you want it. If you don't want it, go and take your chances on the streets'? Perhaps an alternative would be to do some radical rethinking – about the nature of childhood and youth; about the institution of school; about the relationship between living and learning. 'Childhood', 'School', 'Education', 'Knowledge' are social constructs. They can be challenged and changed. If we continue to quibble about whether parents or the state should exercise the most control of the education system in place at the moment, we run the risk of merely tinkering with the problem instead of seeking to solve it.

Activities

Key Questions

Discuss how far the promotion of competition among schools is the best way forward in a state maintained system of education.

Why did central government move to dismantle the system put in place by the 1944 Education Act?

Explain the different roles of the constituent elements making up the so-called 'educational partnership'.

How radical are the changes put in place by the legislation of the eighties and early nineties?

What were, in your opinion, the absolutely key elements of the 88 Act that facilitated the notion of parental choice as bringing pressure to bear upon schools to drive up standards?

In a world of winners and losers, which partner of the 44 dispensation has most lost out? Justify your answer.

What powers did local education authorities enjoy at the beginning of the 1980s? What powers do they now enjoy? Do they have a future? Are they needed?

What are the key powers central government now enjoys over the nation's schooling?

What is the National Curriculum? How is it decided upon? What role does it play in the ambition to raise standards in the nation's schools?

What are the dangers associated with too great an influence of the state in the education of the young?

What role do parents and governing bodies have to play in the governance of our schools?

How have the powers and responsibilities of governing bodies changed from the 44 Education Act?

'Amateurs in a world of professionals'. How far do you think this a fair summary of the role of governing bodies in the lives of our schools under the present legal regime?

Are parents simply a pawn in government policy or do they have a significant role to play in influencing our schools for the better?

What is the reality of parental choice in the schooling of their child?

Are teachers as the professionals in our schools afforded sufficient respect?

Suggestions for Reading

The Law of Education (various editions). The bible in this area. To be found in any self-respecting university library in the reference section. Any piece of educational legislation, government advice in the form of Circular and memoranda, etc. is to found within its ever-expanding volumes.

MacClure, Stewart (latest edition) *Education Re-formed*. London: Hodder & Stoughton. A nice, accessible, balanced and readable account of the changes put into place by central government.

Munn, Pamela (ed.) (1993) *Parents and Schools*. London: Routledge. A very useful set of papers on the parental role and its possibilities in the aftermath of the key legislation. Have a particular look at the paper by Ruth Jonathan, 'Parental Rights in Schooling', which raises fundamental issues about whether the celebration of parental rights in education is necessarily an unqualified good.

Neville, Harris (1993) *Law and Education*. London: Sweet & Maxwell. Inevitably, given the pace of change, this book is already out of date in its legal detail. But it does provide an informed, critical perspective on the themes of regulation and consumerism informing central government attitudes towards the nation's education system. An earlier text by Paul Meredith (1992) *Government, Schools and the Law*. London: Routledge is an equally intelligent piece of writing on the significance of the changes in Education law of the eighties. It is very important to grasp the ideologically charged significance of the changes to our schooling system of the eighties and nineties. Subsequent Labour administrations have simply pursued with (if possible) greater zeal the agenda of change put in place by prior Conservative governments.

Tooley, James (2000) *Reclaiming Education*. London: Continuum. A radical and challenging critique of the present dominant role of the state in education, its provision and standards. A plea is made to set education free from the baleful and counterproductive influence of the state. Important questions are posed and provocative suggestions are put forward as an alternative to the present situation. Well worth reading.

Three other texts worth taking a look at are Gerwitz, S., Ball, S. J. and Bowe, R. (1995) *Markets, Choice and Equity in Education*, Feintuck, M. (1994), *Accountability and Choice in Schooling* and Deem, R., Brehony, K. and Heath, S. (1995), *Active Citizenship and the Governing of Schools* – all are Open University Press publications. Their titles are self-explanatory.

Certainly also to be looked at are government White Papers on Education. See in particular *Choice and Diversity* DFE 1992, *Self Government for Schools* DfEE 1996, and latterly *Excellence in Schools* DfEE 1997.

Suggested Practical Activities

1. Get hold of some local school prospectuses. Analyse them for their content. See if you can tell what elements in the school prospectuses are clearly a requirement of law. Do they all, in other words, make a point of including certain kinds of information even if that information is not necessarily to their benefit? Can you tell from the tone of the prospectuses which schools feel confident in selling themselves to parents? Do they make a point about presentation, how the prospectus looks? Is there any suggestion of some schools being poor relations?

2. If you can, talk to some teachers. Ask them about the school governors. Can they name any of them? Can they list their powers? Do they feel comfortable with the powers that governors have, and in particular the powers governors have over their professional lives?

3. If you can, talk to a couple of head teachers. Ask them how they view the role of governors. Do they find the governors supportive? Are the governors seen as a source of strength to the school? What do individual governors bring to the school that aids the school for which they have responsibility?

4. Ask some parents whether they think they are in partnership with the school their child attends. What does partnership mean to them? Ask them if their expressions of parental choice on which school their child attends were or are being met. What lengths would they go to get their child into their preferred school? And in any event, on what grounds did/will they make their choice?

5. Ask the 'professionals' if they regret the declining power of local education authorities over their schools. Would any of them go back to the pre-1988 days where control of school budgets lay with LEAs rather than the school governing body?

6. Ask your interviewees to list the pros and cons of the existing legal regime affecting the day-to-day life of the schools with which they are familiar.

7. The Secretary of State for Education writes informing you he or she wishes to take stock of the plethora of changes of the last twenty years. Your opinion will be much valued. This is, after all, a listening government (all evidence to the contrary notwithstanding). Write a critical evaluation for the Minister of the merits of the main changes to our schooling system put in place over the last twenty years.

8. A group of young children are demanding a greater say in what they study. They are sick and tired of adults determining what they learn. Are you sympathetic with this potentially very subversive movement demanding a bit less oppression, a bit more self-determination for children? Make your views known in a letter to your local editor.

9. Ian Gregory is clearly anxious about the role of central government in determining curriculum content. Nick McGuinn equally clearly thinks he is making too much of the issue. Who should determine the curriculum? Does it make sense to democratize curriculum decision-making? If it does, how might it be done?

CHAPTER 5

Education for a Better World?

Ian Davies

Introduction

The main purpose of education is to help prepare people to live a better individual life and also to contribute to the improvement of wider society (locally, nationally and globally). As such, education is perhaps best characterized as a moral enterprise. This chapter focuses on those direct and explicit attempts to teach people about issues in contemporary society and to help them to prepare to play an active and positive role in a democracy.

After a brief scene-setting section in which some key terms and issues are clarified, I draw attention to a number of fundamental dilemmas for this form of education. I then give a number of very brief case studies including education that might assist with the achievement of equal opportunities, citizenship, enterprise and sustainability. Finally, I describe some overarching themes that might help teachers and others find a way forward beyond the many difficult challenges that are an essential part of these forms of education.

What are the Key Terms in Education for a Better World?

The working title for this chapter had been 'Education as a Moral Enterprise'. But this was ultimately rejected and it is important to make clear now what this chapter will *not* do. I will not make many comments about the general aims and structure of education systems. Education can make a better world but I am concerned here with a particular type of work that can be seen in action in classrooms rather than in policy statements about the general administrative framework. I will not refer much at all to those general arguments that see the positive contributions that can be made by many individual subjects. Science education is valuable and can help people to understand contemporary society, but for the most part it is still largely concerned with learners' ability to grasp scientific principles within a context rather than to appreciate the nature of society. Finally, I will not concentrate on spirituality or on those issues that relate narrowly to personal matters. I am concerned with attempts to explain the world and not to, on the one hand, think beyond it, or, on the other, to focus on matters such as individual health or friendships.

I am concerned with what is described in countries such as the USA as 'social education'. I want to discuss the issues that surround how students learn how to think and act in ways that will enhance the possibility of achieving a thriving and robust democratic society. To help achieve this aim I need to emphasize one or two starting-points. Freire's assertion needs to be remembered:

> We can never have an educational activity which is a neutral one – no matter whether we as educators are conscious of it or not. I understand in certain societies like yours [he was speaking about England] there is a strong tradition of the neutrality of education – but it is an illusion. It is argued in the name of science, culture, humanity, pretending that we are not [biased]. And if education cannot be neutral it is for domestication, domination or liberation (in Lister, 1973).

This does not mean that we must immediately leap to a narrow-minded approach that tries to identify who is for 'us' and who supports 'them'. It certainly does not mean that all we have to do is to search for some sort of pattern or law that exists under all the heterogeneity of human experience. The nature of 'good' or virtue is of course extremely problematic. Should we emphasize the need to help the majority; to defend what is right in all circumstances; to ensure that cultural matters are interpreted in local contexts or something else when we are deciding what is acceptable? All these terribly difficult matters will certainly not be finally clarified in this chapter or in any other piece of writing. And yet, within the confines of the argument I wish to develop, education for a better world is a form of moral enterprise. That moral enterprise comes to fruition as teachers develop learners' capacities to understand and to develop the need for a commitment to universal human rights within political, economic, social and cultural contexts. The need to develop an awareness of curriculum and pedagogy that characterize these matters is very pressing (Whitty, 1992).

What are the Fundamental Dilemmas in Developing 'Education for a Better World'?

It is necessary to say a little about the nature of the most fundamental issues that are at the heart of debates about education for a better world. Heater (2000) draws attention to four dilemmas facing those who promote citizenship education and I have used his framework to make clear the relevant parameters of the key debates. In line with Freire's comments presented above (and accepting that teachers may not address the dilemmas shown below in an explicit way) no teacher can operate neutrally. My own views are presented so as to make clear my position and I suggest that all teachers who educate for a better world should have an explicit awareness of their own ideas and positions.

First dilemma

Teachers need to be able to find some sort of balance, or at least a reasonable understanding, of the differences between duties and rights. What are students expected to learn: to do what they should do, or to claim what is rightly theirs? Those associated with the civic republican tradition of political thought have tended to stress duties, while liberals tend to favour rights. Either position can be represented negatively or positively. An individual who seeks his or her rights at the expense of others may be acting in an unacceptable manner; but, equally, a state that demands an unreasonable fulfilment of duties in the name of the common good is not acting democratically. For some the traditions may be in conflict. Wolfe (1999, p. 429), for example, has suggested that it has not yet been convincingly argued how 'putting the common good *ahead* of one's private interests is compatible with liberal values such as autonomy'. This would seem to render teaching for a better world to be either partial or contradictory. If this is the case then teachers will face very many challenges to their professional work. But perhaps there are some more positive ways forward. The differences between rights and duties may break down fairly readily. For example, is it my right or my duty to look after my children? It is clearly both. We can argue that:

by being a virtuous, community-conscious participant in civic
affairs (a republican requirement), a citizen benefits by enhanc-
ing his or her own individual development (a liberal objective).
Citizenship does not involve an either/or choice. (Heater, 1999,
p. 177)

Not all will be persuaded by such seemingly attractive compromises
and complete logical clarity cannot be expected. However, the
dilemma of balancing rights with duties should not hinder good
educational work and I believe that the sort of balance offered by
writers like Dagger (1997) and Heater is necessary and valid. Teaching for a better world is difficult but it is possible to work from a
conceptual base that makes sense.

Second dilemma

A second dilemma is concerned with the sort of teaching that should
be practised. Heater (2000) when discussing citizenship asks about
the balance or emphasis that should be placed on civil and political,
or social contexts. Others would extend this argument and argue for
the primacy of moral or spiritual matters. Much of this debate is
linked to the point made above. To take an extreme case, Soviet
Russia made its case for democracy on the supposed achievement of
social and economic rights while arguing that Western-style political
rights did not need to be made real through the ballot box. Again,
the argument can be made more clearly through overstatement. The
very varied collection of countries sometimes referred to as the
'West' do not, in practice, seem to think that there is too much
wrong with a society in which there are huge disparities in wealth
with many living below the poverty line, as long as there is some
sort of conscience-salving safety-net that can be used by some. These
debates are sometimes confused or enriched (depending on one's
perspective) by those who argue for a fuller appreciation of less
material matters. Halstead and Taylor (2000) have recently reviewed
the extensive research into values, attitudes and personal qualities
and some recent research suggests that citizenship is seen in terms of
social and moral concern as opposed to political, social or economic
rights or duties (Davies *et al.*, 1999). My own view here is wrapped
up with a search for an education that seeks always to address
fundamental matters and does not confuse contexts and concepts. In
other words, I prefer to aim for learners to develop conceptual
understanding and relevant skills as opposed to seeking to know
more about specific cases. I would be less interested in promoting

knowledge of, say, the particular case of apartheid South Africa and more concerned to use various case studies (such as South Africa) in the development of a better knowledge of prejudice, discrimination and racism. Furthermore, I do have a preference for developing political understanding over and above other matters. The precise nature of that political understanding requires detailed explanation and will be returned to when I discuss developments in citizenship education.

Third dilemma

The third fundamental dilemma relates more obviously than the points made above to expectations for student behaviour now and in the future. Are learners expected to participate actively in society or to abstain? It would seem initially that the former would be welcomed. The idea of people making positive contributions seems to be a good one, and the political theory associated with participatory democracy gives these feelings a real weight. However, the nature of democracy is not so simple. If we live, or wish to live, in a representative democracy we might want our leaders (who have been elected in a fair way by a knowledgeable public) to get on with the job of governing while we are left with time to pursue other important matters such as earning a living, raising a family and developing worthwhile leisure activities. Arguments can be developed for a healthy democratic society that involve *not* doing things: not breaking the law; not complaining unnecessarily; not being a nuisance to others. Although there is no real evidence for a generational decline in political interest, the voting figures for young people seem to suggest that there is less than full engagement with the constitutional political process (Jowell and Park, 1998). When very positive statements are made about the link that teachers can make between active classroom involvement and anticipated democratic action in later life (Hahn, 1998) it must be understood that a particular (and, relatively new) version of democracy is being promoted. My clear preference here is for participatory behaviour although I do accept that this approach carries many risks and some obvious disadvantages.

Fourth dilemma

The final dilemma goes to the very heart of the educational process. Is it possible to see society in a coherent single framework or are we witnessing such extensive fragmentation of identities, values, cultures and political agendas that any talk of education for a better world is unhelpful? The real nature and extent of globalization is unclear (Green, 1997) but the numbers of references that are made to the decline of the power of the state are extensive. A very wide range of identities that can be held by individuals is now much more explicitly acknowledged (Isin and Wood, 1999). Some would argue that all that is possible is to aim for better worlds that can be inhabited by different learners at different times in different ways. My preference here is for what can be described as a universalist approach. This needs some clarification. Debates have developed (e.g. to do with globalization, post-modernism, feminism) that suggest the uncertainty of knowledge and the need to review the range of responses based on 'local' considerations as opposed to domination by rich Western societies. My view is that the arguments made against universal human rights have only superficial and dangerous attractions. The arguments for universalism must be, in my view, strongly supported. However, it is worth spending a little time on the superficial attractiveness that I have mentioned above. Initially, the arguments for relativism seem to have some force: when Fukuyama (1992) claimed in the aftermath of the collapse of the Berlin Wall that we had reached the 'end of history', his lack of attention to, for example, the rise of Islam showed a staggering Western bias that needs to be balanced. Simplistic claims for the existence of one world cannot be accepted. Indeed, beyond the academic debates held in ivory towers it is outrageous to hear of the disregard of values, traditions and cultures by those who are richer and more powerful.

Of course, in tackling such huge issues in this short space I risk oversimplifying complicated and very diverse positions. My own position cannot be stated strongly as I argue that there will always be a search for truth that proceeds uncertainly in limited stages with interim rather than final points being achieved. However, the relativists have two fundamental weaknesses: their arguments are intellectually weak and politically unacceptable. It cannot be accepted in academic terms that an overarching position is developed with the effect of describing the impossibility of developing an overarching perspective. The relativists' nonsense has been convincingly shown as such by a strong attack from the historian who provided much of the evidence used to show the unacceptability of the historical methods of Irving. The latter became notorious as someone who denied the existence of the Holocaust (Evans, 1997). Secondly, and very strongly related to the first point, is the dangerous practical effect of asserting the impossibility of truth. That irrationality will only favour the imposition by the powerful of their own specific ideas that may be unacceptable but which cannot be challenged by claims against truth. Of course, the domination of that which is not true occurs to some extent already, and a post-modernist position would ensure only that it would happen more frequently (Appleby *et al.*, 1994). Adherence to the notion of universal human rights does not mean that a complete moral theory has been developed. Human rights charters and much of the philosophical thinking on which they are at least in part based are far too sketchy for that. Nor does it mean that there is a guide for action in all cases. There is always going to be a need to think very carefully about what is the best practical way forward when attempts are being made to resolve conflicts. However, a universalist approach is the best way to ensure that a solid and rational search for truth and justice can proceed. Teachers have an important part to play in this enterprise.

How Can 'Education for a Better World' Be Developed?

A number of ways have been suggested to help people study the contemporary world and, in some cases, prepare them to become more effective. I will review some of these attempts using examples from various recent projects and movements. It will, of course, be an incomplete review, being mainly centred on work in England and limited to examples from, roughly, the last three decades. It will cover equal opportunities, citizenship, enterprise and sustainability.

Equal opportunities

The need to promote equality is often regarded as a prime consideration for teachers. I will try to characterize the main elements of the debates and then give some examples from specific areas. The central issue relates to the distinctions that can be drawn between equality of outcome and opportunity. For the latter it may be regarded as sufficient for a level playing field to be established prior to competition taking place. For the latter, there is perhaps a need to ensure as far as possible that benefits and not just opportunities are shared. Perhaps the best way to gain some sort of insight into the characterizations of equal opportunities is to look at the three educational perspectives: multicultural education; gender education; and the social class context.

'Multicultural education' is almost certainly the wrong phrase to use for work that focuses on a variety of issues but it is perhaps the title that is most easily recognized. Prior to the 1960s (although there were exceptions proposed by academics and by some politicians) assimilation was the principal response to the 'problem' of a nation suddenly coming to terms with increased immigration and a wider cultural base than it had previously acknowledged. This would mean that 'we' would host 'them'. The complete unacceptability of this was rather belatedly recognized although not without some strong and perhaps continuing opposition. Underachievement was recognized and explained (e.g. Coard, 1971) although not always acted upon. By the 1970s, however, multicultural education was being discussed and there were efforts to develop a greater awareness among learners of cultural differences. Well-intentioned people often made these attempts and it was encouraging that a high profile government report chaired by Lord Swann published in 1975 strengthened the resolve to promote justice. However, the multicultural education of the 1970s soon became associated with a negative display of colourful costumes and exotic food that changed nothing. It was dismissed as the '3 Ss': saris, samosas and steel bands. This heralded the anti-racism of the 1980s. A harder hitting and politically more demanding programme was developed and was taken up by many, including some influential local education authorities. It found an edge in the Thatcher-dominated 1980s but has all but disappeared in the more consensual contemporary context. The increasing dislike for any title that included the word 'race' may also have been a factor in the decline of anti-racist work. While racism does exist, the concept of 'race' is simply a social construct and its use may, unacceptably, imply some sort of biological link. Schools that served mostly white communities had failed to become involved. The new way of thinking about these matters became associated with intercultural education. Proponents of this form of education looked for changes within the 'host' community as well as elsewhere. It was strongly promoted by the Council of Europe (see Rey, 1997) and it has perhaps become a part of development education.

Gender education is centrally important and has also seen important shifts in its nature. From about 1975 (the date when one author says that 'policy initiatives were first developed to address issues concerning the education of girls' (Martin, 1999, p. 103)) attention was focused on the perceived underachievement of girls. Now the emphasis has shifted on to boys' underachievement, although it is unlikely that the boys have slipped, or the girls achieved, as much as is reported in the media. As such the nature of the debates remains fundamentally around elements of radical or liberal feminism. The latter would be content to see success achieved within existing frameworks. The radicals would perhaps be more likely to see gender groups forming relatively separate interest groups and would more readily acknowledge the significance of what can, in shorthand, be referred to as the politics of everyday life.

Matters relating to social class have also seen many shifting perspectives. In the 1960s a number of seminal works appeared (e.g. Jackson and Marsden, 1966; Halsey *et al.*, 1961; Douglas, 1964) that drew on the experience of working-class grammar school and secondary modern school students. Initially the issues were seen in terms of access. More working-class students had to become more successful. Language and other cultural matters were recognized as being significant but policy initiatives were associated with structural changes that led to comprehensive schools being rapidly increased from about 1965 (although they had existed before that date). However, the language of social class has all but disappeared in recent years. This does not mean that there is no longer any concern about the links between poverty and educational achievement. Also, it should be stressed that a number of books have developed new insights into the relationships between various aspects of equal opportunities. In very different ways both Abraham (1995) and Skeggs (1997) discuss the interrelationships between class and gender so that educational implications are made clear. However, it is now far less likely for class to be seen as an educational issue. This is partly due to the demographic and sociological developments that have seen the disappearance of the traditional working class based in manual jobs in heavy industry. But it is also due to a historical and ideological shift in which there is a greater emphasis on individual action; a replacement of industrially based communities with communitarianism and a rejection of Marxist-related analyses after the fall of the Berlin Wall.

'Race', gender and class are the great themes within the last three decades of educational thinking. And yet they relate often to policy-making in, for example, issues to do with access, and on the other hand provide examples for a programme that examines political matters. It is to political issues that I now turn in a consideration of my preferred framework for education for a better world: citizenship.

Citizenship

Some of what was written in the early part of this chapter relates directly to citizenship and that probably reflects my own feeling that this area is the way in which to most usefully represent what is needed in education for a better world. Citizenship represents a sufficiently powerful and overarching conceptual framework to allow for some very useful educational work. It can encompass many strands of thinking about democratic practices. But in its three central concerns with legal status, identity and capacity for effective and appropriate action it is also effective for limiting key debates. It enables teachers to concern themselves with rights as practised as well as stated; and it enables the separation of examples from fundamental concepts and frameworks. Above all, it prevents unhelpful diversions into, on the one hand, the teaching of dry and misleading constitutional information and, on the other, the over-emphasis on personal matters that can be seen in some personal and social education classes that forever discuss friendship but never explore deeper societal issues. And yet, citizenship has gone through a number of stages, not all of which have been entirely positive. Prior to the 1970s, if anything was done explicitly to teach learners about political matters, it took the form of British Consti-tution courses for high status students. In the 1970s political liter-acy became influential and shifted ideas about teaching on to politics with a small 'p'. In other words, there were discussions about issues, attempts to develop learners' potential for action and a commitment to what were described as 'procedural values' such as respect for truth and reasoning rather than simply giving pupils the 'right' answer (Crick and Porter, 1978). Attention moved in the early 1980s to 'new' or adjectival' educations (peace, anti-racist, development) which were both more related to political pro-grammes (some local education authorities, for example, became very obviously associated with campaigns such as that for nuclear disarmament) and at the same time more holistic and affective, striving to make connections between personal consciousness and the resolution of world issues such as pollution and conservation. By the 1990s, when there was a Conservative government in power, there were concerns about a rising crime rate, and there was an ageing population who were seen largely in negative terms as a burden on the state, young people were encouraged to become active citizens by recognizing their 'voluntary obligations' (Hurd, 1989). This, fortunately, is now being replaced with something far more meaningful and professional. The ambitious aims that are now in place reflect an attempt to transform the political culture (see Crick, 2000) so that citizens are more knowledgeable and better able to participate in political matters. The three key areas are political literacy, social and moral responsibility, and community involvement. It remains to be seen whether changes in the political culture can actually be achieved.

Enterprise education

The title, until recently, of the key government ministry (the Department for Education *and* Employment) suggests that there is an essential link between the economy and the education system. This is both sensible and obvious, and, at the same time, potentially rather alarming. There is on the part of many commentators and politicians a rather simplistic, almost naïve, belief in the relationship between education and economic effectiveness. Perhaps the best-known author who asserts this connection is Barnett (1986) who argues that after World War Two the education system was antipathetic to profit-making industry and commerce. John MacGregor (Education Secretary during the early 1990s) used to refer explicitly to Barnett's work and there has been no shortage of key political advisors who have agreed and urged better performance by schools. Tony Blair's much-trumpeted priority of 'Education, education, education', it can be imagined, owed much to this perspective. Economic considerations have been responsible for the growth in competition between schools and within classrooms. There is now far less emphasis on the intangible outcomes of improved understanding of justice and enhanced dignity and co-operation and rather more to be heard about the desperate 'need' to improve examination performance that signifies the achievement of 'useful' knowledge. Schemes have been developed to allow teachers to experience industrial placements, for learners to undertake work-related projects and for students to understand the direct relationship between wealth creation and benefits for individuals, communities and society (NCC, 1990).

Of course, the picture is not entirely straightforward. The drive for education to be directed towards improved economic performance is rather entangled with a number of other debates. Gray (1998) has suggested that we may face only a false dawn if we imagine that economics can answer our most difficult questions. Rubinstein (1993) further questioned the foundations of the debate by suggesting that the systems of education in the UK had always been well suited to the particular economy that had developed. When chief inspector of Ofsted, Chris Woodhead railed against new courses which seem to be very practical but are perhaps less vocationally worthwhile (in terms of developing skills that can be applied at work) than high status traditional subjects such as English. Dewey (1966), certainly not an advocate of education for the creation of a compliant workforce, declared that he was in favour of vocational education as long as it had the capacity to help transform the system. Critics such as Gleeson (1987) and Bates *et al.* (1984) were opposed to vocational education not because it is unnecessary to develop 'real world' knowledge and understanding but rather that various government schemes grew only at times of unemployment and were designed to occupy rather than educate.

These debates seem to focus on the meaning of the term 'enterprise'. If one sees it as relating only to economic matters and requiring a suspension of critical thinking then it is unhelpful. If, on the other hand, enterprise is seen as requiring a broader perspective that implies a willingness and ability to be innovative in many different ways and contexts within a democratic framework then it may relate very positively to valuable forms of citizenship. It is only the latter formulation that I believe can lead to worthwhile educational work. There is much to resist if politics is replaced by economics and welfare overtaken by consumerism.

Education for sustainability

This area, like others, can be characterized in terms of a continuum. In this case the spectrum runs from the quest for personal peace and harmony to political campaigns against nuclear weapons (largely in the 1970s and 1980s) and for environmentally friendly governmental policies and commercial practices (most noticeably since the 1990s). This brief comment should not be interpreted to suggest that matters are so straightforward. Peace education has a long, largely very respectable and at times establishment-based history (Heater, 1984). Further, the meaning of peace is hugely complex and encompasses, among other frameworks, debates over the need for something more than simply the absence of war. This would relate to concerns about structural violence such as institutionalized racism and the extent to which individual relationships impinge upon other contexts such as globalization. ('Act locally, think globally' is, depending on one's viewpoint, a rather empty slogan or something that encapsulates an important principle and a political rallying cry.)

There have been some very thought-provoking and pedagogically useful publications (e.g. Hicks, 1988; Pike and Selby, 1988). Huckle (1990) gives a good outline of the different strands of environmental education. He refers to the 'technocentrists' who, while largely supporting the status quo, display a managerial approach. This group can be seen as either 'accommodators' who wish to see some limited reform, or 'optimists' who feel that market forces and scientific and managerial ingenuity will be sufficient to ensure the future of the planet. The ecocentrists, on the other hand, argue for more harmonious relations between people and with the environment. They can be divided into 'communalists' (believing in collective self-reliance) and 'Gaianists' (opting for a self-regulating world).

In these hugely complex debates I own to seeing sustainability as being unable to move beyond the category of a theme. It provides examples that help generate political understanding but is insufficiently strong and dynamic to provide a lasting pedagogical framework.

What are the Key Issues for Teachers and Learners?

Throughout the above projects, initiatives and movements there are some common themes. I now attempt to draw attention to those themes and make clear what I believe to be the necessary way forward.

The significance of definitions

In all the above there is a constant sense of existential crisis. 'Who am I?' might be the question most often posed by a teacher who works in this field. This navel-gazing is both absolutely necessary and a huge stumbling block. In an intellectual sense there is a healthy vibrancy about the long-running debates about fundamental matters. It is no surprise that 'What is citizenship?' and 'What is history?' are titles of first rate books that clarify the essence of the humanities, and that corresponding titles for maths and science are conspicuous largely by their absence. What is fundamental and what is 'merely' an example? What is merely fashionable and what is of enduring human concern? Can we look for a set of reasonably common responses when faced with a variety of controversial issues? To what extent is it acceptable to have differences between personal actions and principles that are applied to more general contexts?

There will, however, be a sense in which there is rather too much uncertainty. When I have at various points throughout this chapter toyed with 'humanities', 'citizenship', 'moral enterprise' and 'education for a better world' as useful ways to characterize the range of study, there is rather obviously an attempt to grapple with something that is coming to resemble a many-headed monster. This sort of questioning is necessary but it is, for most, also simply confusing.

In a political context some have argued that this never-ending dispute allows much good work to be done. It shows, some might argue, democratic debate in action. I cannot imagine anyone wanting to accept one way of looking at the political world. At times the swift move from, for example, peace education to global education to futures education as each title came under attack allows the same people to keep doing the same sort of work. And yet, it is not possible to be too positive about uncertainty. The bickering between rival camps has allowed the clearest characterization of these areas to be made by the most powerful (i.e. the government). There has been a lack of 'real world' work in schools and classrooms as people have succumbed to the lure of the philosophical rather than the pedagogical debate. Simply, it is far easier to engage in a rather loose argument around the notion of what we are really here for, as opposed to clarifying the nature of what will be of use when working with teachers and learners.

I need to stress very strongly indeed what I am not arguing. I am not suggesting that we simply need to focus on what 'works'. We should never imagine that we can ignore the nature of our central purposes. We should not look for one single and central response. And yet, we must see 'intellectuals' as teachers and 'teachers' as intellectuals. We must look for co-operative, consensual ways to develop useful work that will lead to the furtherance of a critical, proactive, pluralistic and democratic society. Essentially, this means shifting the emphasis on to educational matters that use insights from other academic disciplines. Without ignoring the political heart of the matter (teachers cannot be neutral) we are travelling into a cul de sac if our central educational purpose is neglected. If the key words of democracy, participation, etc. are regarded as meaning completely different things within an educational context then nothing will be done. This then is not an argument for arguments to end: that would be a crude, undemocratic and unhelpful response. Rather it is for three things to happen: a search for consensus around key *principles* such as those enshrined in human rights documents and an identification of the nature of citizenship; a determination for all those involved in these debates to engage in genuine dialogue (as opposed to be seen as occupying the position of academic or teacher); and a much more explicit focus on pedagogical matters.

Pedagogical goals

In arguing for a much greater emphasis on pedagogical matters it is now necessary to say a little more about what actually should be done. Of course, the range of pedagogical goals is very wide indeed. Should one focus on encouraging people to know more, or being able to do more? What are the limits of critical thinking and what is the point at which active involvement must stop?

An initial response can be given to these difficult matters by considering the structures in which people work. First, there is the school organizational structure that is determined currently by government policy. The debate over comprehensive schools is too complex to be discussed fully here. There will always be exceptions for individual pupils and local circumstances that need to be considered. However, a school system that is built around selection is politically unfair. It is biased towards the wants of the wealthy rather than the needs of the majority and is unsupportable. Second, the ethos of a school is very important. There should be a structure and atmosphere within the school that allows for a reasonable amount of community involvement, dialogue between teachers and between teachers, learners and parents. Perhaps in reality schools cannot be fully fledged democratic institutions but they can be less rigid and authoritarian than they are at the moment. That this is not a utopian dream can be seen in the examples of schools that do valuable work (e.g. Trafford, 1997). Third, the nature of school subjects needs to be considered. Any school that presents one type of knowledge as being isolated from others is deceiving learners. Of course, it is never going to be easy to develop links between subjects. Indeed, recent attempts to establish cross-curricular themes were disastrously unsuccessful (Whitty *et al.*, 1994) and not all the accusations of a lack of rigour that have accompanied such areas as integrated humanities and personal and social education were unjustified. But there are a number of ways forward that allow me to develop the argument more fully into a consideration of a necessary educational process.

Any discussion of a preferred educational process in this area involves three areas: classroom climate; procedural concepts; assessment. The climate within a classroom is closely allied to the issues surrounding the ethos of the school. Unless there is mutual respect between teachers and learners and an opportunity for initiative little of any use will occur. Hahn (1998) has shown that the high levels of political interest and efficacy of Danish students emerge from a context in which the students 'attend schools in which political discussion and participation is practised, and they live in a wider political culture in which political discussion and also participation are also prevalent' (p. 101). At times some commentators have declared that this sort of involvement is really only an opportunity for the teacher to promote biased accounts for his or her own political purposes. Mary Warnock in the 1980s spoke of the 'educational horror stories' that every parent had to tell and various right wing think tanks promoted a view of the teacher as a political activist. More measured and informed comments written following classroom research made it clear that teachers could not indoctrinate students, did not want to do so, and in the views of students were largely concerned to encourage learners to put forward their own opinions. Excellent guidance already exists for the teaching of controversial issues (Stradling, 1984). Teachers can be trusted to be professional. The spectre of unacceptable bias and attempted indoctrination has, however, had a distracting effect on the debates and has perhaps hindered the development of some work.

A closer identification of procedural concepts and a determination to ensure that students made progress in relation to them would perhaps provide a way forward. Procedural (or second order) concepts (such as evidence, interpretation) are distinct from substantive concepts that relate more narrowly to the study of particular issues (such as government or war). I would like to develop the possibility of teachers being able to go beyond asking students to memorize details of specific cases, and also to go further than that and to have students consider the nature of the contexts and substantive concepts which may relate to a number of cases. By identifying these procedural concepts it would be possible to invite students not just to think about citizenship but to think as citizens. Teachers and others would be encouraged to move away from citizenship as 'merely' a goal and allow for the possibility of a clearer identification of what students need to do and how they should think in order to demonstrate effective learning. Such an identification and elaboration would mean that the justification for citizenship education would be more straightforward and the potential for misguided attempts at citizenship education (and alarmist reactions to those attempts) would be reduced.

The third issue, of assessment, follows directly from this consideration of procedural concepts. If there were greater clarity about what in educational terms needed to be addressed then we would have a far better idea of how to assess it. At times assessment has been seen as something which is in opposition to, for example, education for citizenship. Would some people be seen as non-citizens if they failed a course; would assessment and so classification of students into different levels mean that the goals of equality had not been achieved? This opposition can be swiftly dealt with. Assessment has a number of purposes. It is only if we were to regard it as having one narrow purpose (the creation of a final summative judgement which would determine who would have access to positional goods) that the criticisms mentioned above would have any validity. The reality is somewhat different. Assessment can be diagnostic, assisting the teacher to know what to teach next and how to teach it. It can be evaluative in so far as it leads to programme changes. Moreover, it is impossible for teachers and students to avoid assessing each other: 'Are they listening to what I am saying?'; 'Is he/she teaching us properly?' are the questions that are always present in the classroom. Of course, the precise range and nature of assessment activities would need a good deal more work and it is likely that difficult issues remain about the sort of knowledge and skills, and the contexts, in which they have to be exercised. However, assessment is a central part of education and can be developed in positive ways.

Conclusion

This introductory statement for 'education for a better world' has omitted a good deal and has said very little about many significant matters. And yet, I want to draw attention to the fundamental debates that underlie any attempt to educate students about society, give examples of particular types of initiative and make arguments about the sorts of things that need to be done in the future. I do not know if schools can *really* make a difference to young people's lives but it seems hard to avoid the notion that education has a major responsibility to attempt to make the world a better place. Teachers should feel confident about their role in society. They are burdened with goals that seem impossible to achieve but they can and must make a difference, and if they feel they *cannot* do so they should stop trying. If they feel they *should not* do so (to return to Freire's point about neutrality) they are only being disingenuous about their political goals.

Response to 'Education for a Better World?'

Nick McGuinn

Ian Davies ended his chapter with a challenge to teachers. He exhorted them to 'make a difference' by working to create a better world. As I tried to demonstrate earlier in this book, such appeals to the idealism of the teaching force have a long and enduring history (Mathieson, 1975). Teachers themselves seem to accept the idea that theirs is a profession which requires exceptional qualities and commitment. Asked a decade ago to describe the essential qualifications for their job, a sample of 100 English teachers emphasized overwhelmingly the importance of 'personal qualities' such as 'professionalism, charisma, enthusiasm' and 'boundless energy' (Protherough and Atkinson, 1991, p. 21).

I see this same sense of dedication today in the young people whom I interview for places on the teacher-training course here at York. Year after year, applicants tell me how they want to share their love of their subject with their future pupils, or, inspired by some charismatic teacher from their own school days, hope to work the same magic on others. I have yet to hear anybody tell me that they have opted for a career in education because they regard it as safe, secure, financially rewarding or a means of gaining power and social prestige.

If the idealism and commitment of teachers is not in doubt, and if they have been answering the 'call to arms' for over a century now, why does Ian Davies still feel it necessary to issue his challenge today? In my response to his chapter, I want to suggest some possible answers to that question.

As an introduction to my argument – and as a means of demonstrating how some of the issues which Ian Davies raises might translate into real classroom situations – I would like you to consider the following anecdote. A young man moved with his family from his home in Malaysia to a city in the North of England. His first language was not English and he found it difficult to adjust to the linguistic challenges posed by his new environment. Nevertheless, he was eager to enter into the life of the school community and was particularly determined to gain as many examination qualifications as he could. What follows is an extract from a written assignment which the young man submitted for inclusion in his coursework portfolio for the General Certificate of Secondary Education in English. The subject is the death of a younger brother. In the extract below – which is reproduced here as written – the young man describes how he felt while waiting to catch the plane which would fly his brother's corpse back to Malaysia for burial:

> I asked my dad if I could help other people to clean or wash his body. He let me do it. But there was no luck. We was waiting for other people to bring his body. Time went so quick. We have to move on soon. We need to go to London as soon as possible. We can't wait no longer. I was feeling so angrily and sad but I did thought that if I don't go soon, the flight might be cancelled for tomorrow.

How is a teacher to respond to such a piece of writing? You will have to take my word for it when I tell you that the whole story is a most powerful and moving account of a personal tragedy. To suggest that it might be altered – still less 'improved' – seems at the very least insensitive. And yet the young man deliberately brought this text into a public space. He asked for it to be judged and graded according to examination criteria. Measured objectively against the conventions of formal written Standard English, this piece of writing would be penalized for its errors of idiom, tense, number and spelling.

Teachers faced with the task of responding to such a text would find themselves confronting the first of Ian Davies' four dilemmas:

> What are students expected to learn: to do what they should do, or to claim what is rightly theirs?

The young author of this text engages, implicitly, with the 'key areas' of 'social and moral responsibility and community involvement' which Davies identifies as fundamental to contemporary thinking about citizenship. Viewed from a moral and philosophical perspective, the story articulates those timeless and universal emotions of grief, bewilderment and anger which human beings feel when a loved one dies:

> I ran inside to find the ambulance and I found the ambulance at the back door. I looked at my parents. I went near them and they've said the words that I hit [hate?] to heard and I will not forget all my life. He had passed away. I started to cried and I could not believe this is happening to me.

Equally important to the protagonist of the story, however, is the need to discharge his moral, religious and civic obligations to his dead brother. The body must be washed and prepared in the approved manner; it cannot be interred on foreign soil but must be flown back to Malaysia for burial:

> . . . we went to our village . . . That night we did a prayer for him and at nine thrithy we interred him. Before that I did touch him for the last time ever in my life.

Reading this text, teachers concerned with education for a better world might feel they had found an ideal student, someone sensitive to core 'substantive values' of piety and obligation; someone who, as Ian Davies puts it, has 'learnt what they should do'. What opportunities this young man's story offers for a serious attempt to 'explain the world'! What possibilities for engagement and development might such a student offer the school and the wider community beyond!

The author of this text, however, had other priorities on his mind. Of course he wished to record his deeply felt testament to his brother; but he did not feel a need to talk about the contents of his narrative with his teacher. What he actually wanted to do was, in Ian Davies' phrase, 'claim' what he felt to be 'rightly his': an objective examination mark and a clear, authoritative explanation of how he could improve his command of written English.

The point of my anecdote is that different people have different ideas about what 'a better world' might actually be. This is why educationalists are faced with the four dilemmas described by Ian Davies in the opening pages of his chapter. Consider, for example, his 'second dilemma' which is 'concerned with the sort of teaching that should be practised'. Ian Davies observes:

> Heater (2000) when discussing citizenship asks about the balance or emphasis that should be placed on civil and political, or social contexts. Others would extend this argument and argue for the primacy of moral or spiritual matters.

Had I, in my role as teacher concerned to promote a 'better world', been asked to respond to the young man's story quoted above, it would have been the narrative's concern for 'moral and spiritual matters' which would have engaged me most strongly, because they are closely bound up with my personal vision of what 'a better world' should be. So how should I react when the author makes it clear, politely but firmly, that he does not regard the classroom as an appropriate place for exploring the issues of morality, obligation, pain and loss raised by his story? If I as teacher am to play any part at all in helping him achieve *his* vision of 'a better world', must I let his concerns take priority over mine? To use Ian Davies' terms again, this young man believes that the teacher's role is to help him engage with the 'civil and political' contexts of citizenship by granting him access to the power of literacy. Who is to say that this is not one of the most compelling of those issues which, Davies tells us, 'surround how students learn how to think and act in ways that will enhance the possibility of achieving a thriving and robust democratic society'?

The practical implications of this concession for me as teacher, however, are that I must respond to the narrative as the young man wants me to – by correcting the syntactical and grammatical errors in his text, no matter how unpalatable such action might seem. Should a teacher give ground like this? Ian Davies' 'third dilemma' poses the question: 'Are learners expected to participate actively in society or to abstain?' One could argue that, since it was the young man himself who brought the concerns raised by the story of his dead brother into the social space of the classroom – a classroom within which the exploration of 'moral or spiritual matters' is regarded as integral to the process of 'education for a better world' – he has an obligation to respect the ethos of that classroom. To expect him to talk about the specific circumstances of his story would be perverse and grossly insensitive; but does that give him the right to abstain from an exploration of what Ian Davies would call the 'concepts' behind the particular 'context', to explore with classmates and teacher, for example, that basic need which, since the time of Sophocles' heroine Antigone, has driven human beings to try to make sense of death through the pious and painful observation of funeral rites?

I, in my role as a teacher concerned with 'education for a better world', want to treat the young man's story as the starting-point for a journey of discovery, one which will help us 'explain the world' to ourselves and to each other in ways that emphasize our common humanity. The young man, however, regards his story not as a beginning but as an act of closure. Should he wish to dwell upon it further, he will do so at home, perhaps, or in the mosque – but certainly not in this classroom. How can two well-meaning people, who both have individual visions of what a 'better world' might be, differ so markedly in their response to the same text? To understand this, we must consider Ian Davies' 'fourth dilemma':

> The final dilemma goes to the very heart of the educational process. Is it possible to see society in a coherent single framework or are we witnessing such extensive fragmentation of identities, values, cultures and political agendas that any talk of education for a better world is unhelpful?

One could certainly forgive teachers for responding to the second part of Ian Davies' question with a despairing 'yes'. As the philosophical, religious and political certainties of the past collapse, so it becomes harder for people to find common ground – literally. Eight years ago, a Conservative Prime Minister described his vision of England: 'The long shadows falling across the county ground, the warm beer, the invincible green suburbs, dog lovers and pools fillers . . . old maids bicycling to Holy Communion through the morning mist' (Quoted in Atkinson, 1995, p. 3). Even as we laugh at such an eccentric description of contemporary England, we cannot help but feel a twinge of sympathy for the sense of loss, the longing for former certainties, which inspired it. Nick Tate, former Chief Executive of the Qualifications and Curriculum Authority, has articulated this concern:

> In England, we have . . . complex problems of identity to solve: our relationship with the United States in a culture that is highly distinct from that of the USA but at the same time massively influenced by it; an ambitious attitude towards European co-operation and integration; all sorts of legacies from our imperial past; and a belated recognition that England is not the same as the United Kingdom and that new relationships need

to be developed between the various parts of the British Isles. (Tate, 1999, p. 15)

It is not only a question of losing a sense of cultural, geographical and political identity, however – significant though those losses are. The very way in which we perceive the world has, in the past half century, been radically challenged. The authority and integrity of that essential tool of communication, language itself, have been shaken both figuratively (by post-modern theories of reading which stress the essential instability of the relationship between signifier and signified) and physically (by the replacement of the typesetter's print-face with the computer programmer's pixel). In a world where 'the long reign of black-and-white textual truth has ended' (Boltor, 1991, p. 2), why should not every word become a plaything, every action and attitude relative and therefore justifiable? One can well understand why Ian Davies, with his concern for universal truths and values, should view the encroachments of relativism with disquiet. Taken to its extreme, the relativist path would lead us, not to a better world, but into a landscape of nightmare:

> All too easy is the neglect or even the dismissal of a natural and historical reality that ought not to be neglected or dismissed . . . For if one adopts, in a cavalier and single-minded fashion, the view that everything is discourse or text or fiction, the realia are trivialized. Real people who really died in the gas chambers at Auschwitz or Treblinka become so much discourse. (Megill, 1985, p. 345)

Ian Davies' concerns are shared by contemporary policy-makers. Nick Tate's speech (quoted earlier) continues with an attack upon 'postmodernism':

> . . . that pervasive relativistic view of the world . . . which sees everything as some kind of a construct: artificial, ephemeral, the result of choices and structures that come and go and in which no authority resides. It is, in addition, a consequence of the democratisation of dominant cultures and of exposure to a multitude of images and influences from other cultures and lifestyles, under the influence of mass global communication. (Tate, 1999, p. 13)

It seems ironic that the politicians who share Ian Davies' unease about the influences of relativism or post-modernism should, by taking steps to counter them, have contributed to the marginalization of those educational concerns which he values most. The Education Reform Act of 1988 provided a rare opportunity to rethink, radically, our ideas about teaching and learning. Instead, the National Curriculum 'compartmentalized' knowledge within traditional subject boundaries and ordered those subjects according to a strict hierarchy of importance. English, Science and Maths, for example, were given top status and awarded the title of 'core' subjects. 'Foundation' subjects such as History and Geography, on the other hand, were placed lower down the order. At least the foundation subjects still had some academic standing. The areas of learning most explicitly concerned with education for a better world – such as citizenship, for example – were marginalized as 'cross-curricular themes, skills and dimensions'.

Nobody opposed to multicultural or gender education, say, actually rails against them openly – apart, perhaps, from a few right-wing extremists. The process of marginalization is much more subtle than that. As John White observed at the time of the introduction of the National Curriculum:

> A most powerful way of indoctrinating pupils is by so organising their studies that certain kinds of reflection . . . are off the agenda. (White, 1989, p. 62)

This is how it is done. A market-driven culture is established so that schools are obliged to compete with each other for pupils and, consequently, for funding. Academic achievement is chosen as the main criterion of success; and this in turn is measured by examinations, the results of which are published in the local and national press. Schools which wish to promote Ian Davies' principles of 'mutual respect', 'opportunity for initiative' and concern for 'procedural concepts' through citizenship education, for example, find themselves in an increasingly untenable position. Unless they invest their resources in the core and foundation subjects, they run the risk of examination failure – with all the negative consequences that would entail. In order to maximize examination potential, pupil groups need to be reorganized according to academic rather than moral or even pastoral criteria. In order to cover the examination syllabus requirements in the short amount of time available, opportunities for speculation, discussion, sustained exploration have to be abandoned in favour of more 'transmissive' modes of teaching and learning.

One fall-back position which teachers committed to the principles of 'education for a better world' might adopt in these circumstances is to try to find a home for their pedagogy and practice within the boundaries of the core and foundation subjects of the National Curriculum. This kind of approach is typified by the following comment: 'Citizenship demands that pupils be taught to use their imagination to consider other people's experiences. What is this but literature and drama?' (Rowberry, 2001, p. 8). The problem with this approach is that it is only partially effective. To return to the young man's story described at the start of my response: if I were to read that text from the perspective of an English teacher rather than, say, a teacher of citizenship, a whole series of concerns which I did not mention earlier would be brought into play. I would, for example, engage closely with the elements of cohesion which bind the narrative at word, sentence and whole-text level. I would consider the way in which the author works a series of binary opposi-tions – life and death, England and Malaysia, sleep and wakefulness, night and day – into the 'edifice' of the text. And so on. The point is, these considerations would distract my attention as teacher from a concentrated meditation upon those 'substantive' and 'procedural' concepts implicit in the text which a 'citizenship reading' would regard as central.

So where does this leave the idealistic teacher committed to 'education for a better world'? It seems that we live increasingly in an educational environment in which only that which can be meas-ured is regarded as important. Perhaps the young man who insisted that his narrative be assessed and graded recognized that fact. Is it significant that he wrote his story as a contribution to his examin-ation coursework in a traditional academic subject, not in response to a citizenship or a personal, social and moral education lesson? If 'education for a better world' is to be taken seriously, do teachers who believe in it need to start to 'play the assessment game' themselves? It sounds ridiculous – offensive, even – to contemplate 'measuring' in some way the sense of piety and moral obligation demonstrated so powerfully by the author of the story. But this does not mean that we should not start to think seriously about the 'substantive' and 'procedural' concepts which underpin his text. What sense of moral or civic obligation, for example, *might* we expect from an average pupil at ages 7, 11, 14 and 16? By what criteria would we measure that pupil's progress? Perhaps it is time that we heeded the 30-year-old advice of Robert Witkin (1974) and thought about how we might nurture and even educate an 'intelli-gence of feeling'.

Ian Davies has issued us with a serious and difficult challenge. I

Activities

The range of ideas and issues covered in Chapter 5 is so large that I have decided to concentrate in this section largely, although not exclusively, on citizenship education.

Key Questions

What is the nature of the relationship between education and a better world?

There are a number of possibilities: education for personal growth; a focus on individual cognitive acceleration; a desire to prepare students directly to make a contribution to society. In this chapter I suggested the need to focus on citizenship education. Is this acceptable?

What is citizenship education?

What is your response to the four dilemmas mentioned in my chapter? If citizenship education was implemented:

- Would it emphasize duties or rights?
- Would it concentrate on social, economic or political matters?
- Would you expect students to become more involved in society as a result of citizenship education or would that lead, unacceptably, to students being forced to participate?
- What sort of values (universalist or relativist) should be emphasized?

How could citizenship education be implemented?

What sort of processes would be appropriate?

- Who should decide what is studied? (Is this the responsibility of the teacher as expert or should there be some negotiation? Are there essential elements that cannot be omitted, e.g. should there be some consideration of local, national and global citizenship?)
- How should teaching and learning take place? (is it, for example, necessary for at least an element of collaborative learning to occur?)
- What should the assessment procedure look like? (The simple memorization of information would probably not be appropriate but would oral testing or an evaluation of an active project necessarily be more suitable?)

Suggestions for Reading

Crick, B. (2000) *Essays on Citizenship*. London: Continuum. Bernard Crick was the chair of the advisory group on Education for Citizenship and the Teaching of Democracy in Schools. The report from that committee has had far-reaching influence and led principally to the introduction of citizenship into the National Curriculum. He was heavily involved in the development and promotion of political literacy in the 1970s and wrote the modern classic *In Defence of Politics* (also published by Continuum). This book contains a variety of his pieces written over a period of almost 30 years.

Dewey, J. (1916/1966) *Democracy and Education*. London: Free Press/Macmillan. Many contemporary debates refer implicitly to Dewey's work. He wrote that he wanted to 'detect and state the ideas implied in a democratic society and to apply these ideas to the problems of the enterprise of education'.

Heater, D. (1999) *What is Citizenship?* Cambridge: Polity Press. Heater explains in a very clear manner the key debates about citizenship today. He has clear preferences but he also allows the reader to see alternatives. This is the best contemporary overview of the fundamental issues in citizenship.

Lawton, D., Cairns, J. and Gardner, R. (eds) (2000) *Education for Citizenship*. London: Continuum. This is an interesting and valuable collection of papers that were originally presented at a conference held at the Institute of Education, London. That conference provided an opportunity for those active in the field to present their thinking and suggestions for practice.

Marshall, T. H. (1963) *Citizenship and Social Class*. London: Macmillan. Marshall was a sociologist who gave an overview of the development of citizenship. He explained that citizenship has a number of different elements that were developed at particular points. Civil aspects became important in the eighteenth century; political aspects in the nineteenth; and social aspects during the twentieth. Marshall is regarded as being highly influential in the development of current educational initiatives.

Pike, G. and Selby, D. (1989) *Global Teacher, Global Learner*. London: Hodder & Stoughton. There are many different conceptions of citizenship. It is useful to look at a way of approaching citizenship that emphasizes the global and moves much further away than others from constitutions and institutions. There are some very good ideas for classroom work. The book has become an educational bestseller as it is seen by teachers as providing both stimulating ideas and valuable practical ways forward.

Reeher, G. and Cammarano, J. (eds) (1997) *Education for Citizenship: Ideas and Innovations in Political Learning*. Oxford: Rowman & Littlefield. Service learning or community involvement is seen as one of the most common ways to implement citizenship education. In this book examples are given of initiatives that 'will enhance citizenship, foster a sense of connectedness to a community stretching beyond the university, and, ultimately, support the practices, basic values and institutions necessary for the democratic process'.

Suggested Practical Activities

1. In his response to my statement about education for a better world Nick McGuinn gives an example of a piece of work included in a GCSE portfolio for English. Nick McGuinn asks 'How is a teacher to respond to such a piece of writing?' Discuss, with others if possible, the responses that could be given and the issues that are raised. What sort of response would you give if you were the teacher?

2. Investigate the meanings that are given to the word 'citizenship'. Ask three people 'what comes to mind when you hear the word "citizenship"?' Also review a national newspaper for one week noting the use of the word 'citizenship'. What sort of ideas and issues are mentioned? Is citizenship seen as something that happens locally and is about morality or are other perspectives included?

3. Read the following scenario and answer the question that follows:

You are the parent of a 12-year-old pupil at a comprehensive school. One of the teachers has recently suggested that your child's class should undertake a role-play exercise in which a randomly chosen group of pupils will experience discrimination. The teacher has explained that discrimination is both so evil and so common-place in today's society that students need to think about and carefully consider the practice associated with prejudice. You can see some benefits that might emerge from this exercise but also have some reservations. Some of your doubts are related to the stated purpose of the exercise itself; some are to do with your feelings about the difficulties that your child may face.

What questions do you need to ask the teacher to be able to make a judgement about whether to allow your child to take part in the exercise?

4. A school is planning to introduce assessment of citizenship edu- cation. The head teacher has argued that without a proper assessment framework citizenship education will be undervalued. The head has explained that it is essential that a particular form of assessment must be developed so that it is appropriate for citizenship education. The head has said in a staff meeting that he does not want to have multiple choice tests about the consti- tution but instead that he wants pupils' understanding, skills and dispositions to be recognized. What sort of assessment framework will be appropriate?

5. Two local schools have begun to work collaboratively. One of the schools achieves excellent academic results; the other is a success- ful special school for pupils with learning difficulties. Both schools pride themselves on a range of achievements. The schools are in some ways similar but one of the key ideas behind the project was to bring people from different communities together so that they could help and learn from each other. The pupils have combined to work together on a citizenship education project about education. They have been encouraged by teachers to ask critical questions about education. The local education authority announces that the special school is to close in the next two years and all pupils will be sent to the local comprehensive. This move is justified by the need to ensure that all students can work more effectively together. The students from the special school are very distressed about this development. All pupils want to protest to the local council. What should the teachers do? Should they support direct action by pupils? Will the pupils seem to be in favour of a rather illiberal segregation?

of education that they cannot be omitted; we do want to make it clear that thinking about education should be rooted in something more than rhetoric.

The second way in which we want to take readers further is by challenging them (yet again) to do more than respond to our debates with a simplistic answer. It is perhaps to be expected that some readers when faced by different opinions will be drawn towards conflicting arguments. We want to urge our readers to go further than responding to a debate by saying something like: 'Yes, both positions appear to be reasonably attractive or persuasive or coherent. The answer must be rooted somewhere in the middle of those arguments. It must be a "bit of both".' Now, that is not to argue that different positions cannot be held simultaneously. We operate on a daily basis with multiple realities. Is education policy sensible? Are school students making progress? 'Yes and no' is obviously the right response but it is not a sophisticated one. We need to identify the parameters of the argument, the criteria for the response, and the nature of the context in which our answers can be applied. Some sort of reference to the work of established 'great educators' might allow us to strengthen and deepen our thinking about education.

We made some comments in the introduction to this book about the nature of our list of great educators. There is no need to repeat those ideas here but it should be emphasized that the list we provide is a mere starting-point and we are rather painfully aware of the absence of contemporary figures. (A fuller list of great educators that we have found useful is provided by the International Bureau of Education, and can be viewed online at www.ibe.unesco.org.) The people who we have included are there following only a rough estimate of who we think 'matters'. But once the list is there we need to consider what, if anything, these people have in common. Rusk (1985) in a very popular book first published in 1918 said that five factors mark the great educator: each contributed theories to the process of education; all had ideas rooted firmly in a definite philosophical position; each brought new ideas forward; their work had practical impact; and, they were seen as being influential over a long period of time. This gives rise to a number of confusing issues. First, our list of great educators overlaps partly but by no means fully with Rusk's preferences. We have space, as he does, for Plato, Rousseau, Montessori and Dewey but here the similarities end. Some 'great' educators perhaps do not have such a long-lasting influence. Second, the lives of individuals are normally used in that they are somehow representative. In other words we can develop a position that asserts the greatness of these individuals only immediately to undercut it with an opinion that the reason why they are interesting is simply because their views tell us something about the wider society. Unless we feel that the power of these individuals was so significant that they are virtually solely responsible for changing the way in which education was thought about and practised then we are left with 'mere' representatives. What is a great educator? Is it someone who merely mirrors or illuminates an existing consensus? Third, and related to the above points, the mode of analysis encouraged by a concentration upon individuals seems to imply a downgrading of social, economic and political forces. Once we start to believe that education can be made by great men (and we use the word deliberately in the light of the list we have chosen – there is only one woman) then we are perhaps neglecting a more sophisticated understanding.

So, with some trepidation and many reservations, here is our list:

Jerome Bruner (1915–   )

Jerome Seymour Bruner was born on 1 October 1915 in New York. His father was a watch manufacturer who died when Bruner was 12 years old. Having gained a doctorate in psychology from Harvard in 1941, Bruner joined the army, serving as an expert on psychological warfare. Returning to Harvard at the end of the war in 1945, Bruner was appointed, first to a professorship in psychology in 1952 and then, eight years later, to the directorship of the university's Centre for Cognitive Studies, a post which he held for twelve years. Between 1972 and 1980, Bruner was professor of experimental psychology at Oxford. On his return to New York, he became professor at the New School for Social Research and a fellow of New York University's Institute for the Humanities.

Bruner developed Piaget's theories of cognitive development, giving them a practical classroom application. By focusing on cognition – the study of thinking as opposed to willing or feeling – Bruner helped to move the emphasis in educational psychology away from the behaviourist model which was dominant in the sixties. Like Montessori, Bruner believes that children have an innate desire and capacity for learning. Like Vygotsky, he argues that it is the task of the teacher to identify the particular stage a child has reached in its cognitive development and, having done so, to help that child move on to the next, 'contingent' stage by 'scaffolding' a further intellectual task in a way which is at once challenging yet not beyond its capacity. As the child grows in confidence, so the teacher can gradually remove the supportive structures of the 'scaffold', encouraging the child to engage in the 'constructivist' process of discovering new ideas or concepts based upon its current or past knowledge.

Bruner described three stages by which human beings represent the environment to themselves when they are learning. The first stage is *enactive representation* which involves learning by doing. The second stage is *iconic representation* which is concerned with the use of pictures, diagrams and patterns to help us remember things we have experienced. The third stage is *symbolic representation*. This is the most sophisticated of the three levels, because it depends upon human beings agreeing to accept an arbitrary, symbolic connection between object and representation. Language is the most obvious example of symbolic representation. Others might include chemical and mathematical formulae.

Bruner also suggested the idea of the 'spiral curriculum', in which the same concept is revisited several times at progressively deeper levels of engagement. This idea has proved particularly helpful to those who would question linear models of progression in learning, such as those laid down in the National Curriculum for England and Wales.

Further reading about Bruner
Olson, D. R. (ed.) (1980) *The Social Foundation of Language and Thought: Essays in Honor of Jerome S. Bruner*. New York: Norton.

John Dewey (1859–1952)
Dewey was born in Vermont, USA, took his PhD with a thesis on 'Kant's Psychology' in 1884, was briefly a school teacher and spent most of his most productive time at the University of Chicago (1894–1904) where he established a famous laboratory school. He is often considered to be the founding father of progressive education and the root of much that is wrong with an unfocused American education system (see Bloom, 1987) but this is a gross simplification if not a straightforward distortion of his work. This criticism of Dewey probably arises from (according to the title of his best-known work) his emphasis on *Democracy and Education* which was first published in 1916. In fact probably the central theme of his work is the desire to challenge supposed opposites. He attacked both traditionalists who wanted to impose knowledge on to children and the groups that wanted children to grow up and be educated 'naturally'. He felt that 'for both children and adults, thinking was an instrument for solving the problems of experience, and knowledge was the

accumulation of wisdom that such problem solving generated' (Westbrook, 1993, p. 279). Teachers, in his view, had to be extremely gifted. They need to be experts in subject knowledge, knowledgeable about child psychology and able to use stimulating teaching methods so that learning subjects would become a part of a child's experience. The titles of his books reflect this desire for unity: *The School and Society; The Child and the Curriculum; Experience and Education; Democracy and Education.* Emphasizing this unity was according to Dewey a way of allowing children to learn democratically and to be prepared for making contributions to the further development of a democratic society. There is no doubt about the impact of his ideas. Debates about his work take place today. Whether or not he is properly represented in those debates is another matter. Furthermore, his attempts to have a direct and immediate impact on school students' lives failed as his laboratory school was forced to close in 1904, ironically as a result of a struggle over workers' rights.

Paulo Freire (1921–1997)

Born in Recife, Brazil, Freire became internationally renowned for his work with and for the poor and oppressed. The main practical focus of his work was on the fight against illiteracy. He was brought up in a Catholic middle-class family, worked with underprivileged people and was exiled in 1964 for his methods of working. He travelled widely and became influential in countries as diverse as the USA, Switzerland and various African states. His key book is *Pedagogy of the Oppressed*. Although he had experienced imprisonment and exile for his work in the earlier part of his life, Freire occupied a significant political position for a short period of time. In 1989 he became Secretary of Education in São Paulo (he resigned following difficulties in 1991).

Freire is mainly associated with work with illiterate people. He believed that it was not enough to learn words but rather that the cultural and economic conditions in which words were used were highly significant. His approach to learning developed into a number of stages: the educators observe the participants to learn what could be needed; appropriate words and themes are identified that will be suitable for literacy work; the words are shown as visual images to help people identify their own culture; the differences in culture between man and animal are explained; dialogue between teacher and learner takes place; and through discussion learners move from 'objects' to 'subjects' of their own destiny (Gerhardt, 1993). The key term for this work is conscientização or consciousness-raising. This is a long way from debates about phonetics or whole books and his ideas caught the imagination of many throughout the world. There are many, however, who make strong criticisms of his work. His tortuous prose remained incomprehensible to many who wanted to hail him as the key figure in the fight against illiteracy. His willingness to join established political institutions seemed at odds with his revolutionary fervour. There is no clear evidence for whether his methods actually led to sustained increases in literacy. By the time of his death in 1997 the world seemed to have moved on and the *Pedagogy of the Oppressed* caused less excitement. But he is still seen today as the most significant educationalist of recent years.

John Locke (1632–1704)

The first of the triumvirate of undeniably great philosophers who became known as the 'British Empiricists'. The others whose names are indelibly linked with Locke are Bishop Berkeley (1685–1753) and David Hume (1711–1776). Locke was educated at Westminster School and Christ Church Oxford. He studied and taught subjects such as moral philosophy, logic, Greek and rhetoric. In keeping with the more polymathic nature of the times, he was particularly interested in matters of medicine. He became, partly as a consequence of the latter interest, Secretary to the Earl of Shaftesbury. This inevitably involved him in the Protestant politics of the time. He had to go into exile in Holland for a period of six years from 1683 to 1689. After the ascension to power of William of Orange he returned to Britain and continued his public life.

As an empiricist, Locke believed that the source of knowledge is experience, and it is experience that is the test of what is known. Experience encompasses what comes via our five senses as well as knowledge coming to us via a looking inwards to the contents and operation of the experiencer's own mind. All of this has the implication that the only way to find something out is to go and look. It is only the use of our senses that can generate knowledge of how the world is. In Locke's famous phrase the mind is a 'tabula rasa' (blank slate).

His most extended thought on education is to be found in 'Some Thoughts Concerning Education' written during the 1680s. They take the form of a series of letters written to friend giving him advice about the kind of training he should give his son. There is no doubt that Locke disliked his own schooldays and was happy to criticize the pedagogical and curricular practices of his day. His own experience as a tutor to Lord Ashley's son influenced his thoughts about the early care and training of children.

The essay falls into two parts; the first concerns itself with the care and training of the child, the second with the education of the young man. Contrary to Rousseau he always thought the education of the child should be directed to the adult the child will become. He saw education as a continuous process. Great emphasis is laid on exercise, the need for sleep, an appropriate diet, an encouragement of a certain hardiness in the child. While very young, children should be taught to be civil to their 'inferiors' and kind to animals.

Children learnt by doing. Beatings serve no useful point. Teaching according to formula is counterproductive if the ambition is quality learning. While there was a place for corporal punishment it should be reserved for persistent cases of 'ill natured behaviour'. The child should be brought initially to recognize the authority of the parent but this relationship of unhesitating obedience should over time be replaced by one of friendship.

Sons should be virtuous, wise, have breeding, have learning. The first three are the most important. Learning is important only if it contributes to a useful and pleasant life in the society within which the son's life is to be passed. Inflicting useless knowledge upon the child, getting him to engage in mindless feats of memorization, serves no significant point, Locke thought. Education should be a convivial activity.

In all kinds of ways Locke's writings on education speak to the modern reader. They repay careful attention.

Maria Montessori (1870–1952)

Born at Chiaravalle, Italy, on 31 August 1870, Maria Montessori was the first woman in Italy to graduate in medicine, receiving her degree from the University of Rome in 1894. Over the next twelve years, she remained in the Italian capital, establishing her medical career. She was director of the State Orthophrenic School from 1899 to 1901 and held a Chair in pedagogic anthropology at the university between 1904 and 1908.

Having successfully established her first 'Casa dei Bambini' for 60 Roman slum children aged 3 to 6 in 1907, Montessori devoted the rest of her life to the development and dissemination of her educational ideas and teaching methods. She travelled around the world, lecturing and offering training. Appointed Government Inspector for Schools in Italy during the early 1920s, Montessori fell foul of

Mussolini's fascist regime and fled first to Spain and then to Holland. She was interned during the war years in India and took this opportunity to develop her movement on the sub-continent, winning the support of Ghandi. After the war, Montessori resumed her work of dissemination. Her movement grew steadily and she received international acclaim. Towards the end of her life, she was nominated for the Nobel Peace Prize three times. She died at Noordwijk in the Netherlands on 6 May 1952 at the age of 81.

Montessori's approach to education was inspired by her experiences at the Orthophrenic Clinic in Rome where she worked with mentally retarded children. Influenced by the ideas of two French doctors, Jean Itard and Edouard Seguin, she discovered that, given guidance and stimulation in a carefully structured environment which was at once challenging yet supportive, children who had been dismissed as uneducable could make dramatic progress. She quickly realized that her teaching methods could be applied successfully to young learners of all abilities and backgrounds.

Fundamental to Montessori's approach is a belief in the individual child's innate capacity for initiative, creativity and discovery. She saw the role of the teacher – or 'director' – as essentially low-key. The director's task was to establish the conditions in which individual learning might flourish. Using physical materials such as beads, wood and sandpaper to stimulate the intellectual curiosity and conceptual understanding of young learners, the 'director' would guide the student through what Montessori described as the 'periods of sensitivity' which mark the various stages of the learning process. (Like Piaget, who supported her work, Montessori believed that intellectual and biological development are connected.)

Montessori had no time for the didactic, transmission approach to education which sees young learners as empty vessels to be filled with the received wisdom of adulthood. As she memorably put it, such an approach was tantamount to treating children as if they were so many butterflies waiting to be pinned to the wall of convention and compliance.

Further reading on Montessori
Standing, E. M. (1957) *Maria Montessori: Her Life and Work*.
London: Hollis & Carter.

A. S. Neill (1883–1973)
Neill was brought up in a strict family dominated by Calvinism. He was an individualist who spent almost his whole life as a pupil or

teacher or head teacher. His most famous achievement is the establishment of Summerhill School which opened in 1924 and which
still exists (run by his daughter), despite the attention of government
inspectors. Although he wrote many books, his ideas are probably
most clearly articulated in the 1962 work, *Summerhill: A Radical
Approach to Education.*

His methods are seen as a strong promotion of freedom and self
expression for pupils. In fact his school became known as the place
where there are no rules; or, at least, where the rules are established
by the pupils as much as the teachers (Saffrange, 1994). Although
he rejected the negative and repressive characteristics of Calvinism,
his work owes much to a religious and possibly Christian outlook.
He values the innate goodness of people, believing that if left to
their own devices they will create more happiness and reveal more
potential than if forced to do what others say. This outlook also
relates to psychoanalytical perspectives. It is possible that the greatest influences on Neill are Homer Lane (who established a similarly
free-thinking school) and Wilhelm Reich. He was also influenced by
Freud, and there is an element of a desire to get beyond the
repression that has sexual connotations in his work. It was only the
threat of closure that led Neill to tell pupils that sexual relationships
were not to be tolerated.

He appears not so much a philosopher or psychologist and more
of a libertarian dreamer. His books as well as reported conversations
suggest that he was less willing to engage in rigorous justifications
for his work, resorting instead to anecdotes about various pupils that
he had known. The emphasis on freedom is possibly at odds with his
own highly individualized charismatic leadership and the need for a
community to be created in a certain way. The viability of his
methods for all but a tiny minority who can afford to seclude
themselves in the English countryside must be questioned strongly.

The boundaries between education and therapy are thrown into
relief by the work of Neill and it is not entirely clear if an effective
educational programme can be established or if most students who
attend lessons would actually find rather traditional methods being
used. Neill created a school that has survived many challenges for a
very considerable period of time. At a time when uniformity seems
to characterize much of what happens in education there is perhaps
a pressing need for reference to be made to the work of individuals
like Neill who present us with alternatives.

Jean Piaget (1896–1980)

Jean Piaget was born in Neuchatel, Switzerland. His first academic interest was zoology and he developed a precocious talent for it, making his name as a scholar by the age of 15. Having gained a doctorate in zoology from the University of Neuchatel in 1918, Piaget was drawn to psychology. He pursued this new interest by moving first to Zurich to study with Carl Gustav Jung and Eugen Bleuler and then, in 1919, to the Sorbonne at Paris. Two years later, Piaget took up the post of Director of the Institut Jean-Jacques Rousseau in Geneva, returning, five years later, to the University of Neuchatel where he became professor of philosophy. Piaget joined the faculty of the University of Geneva as professor of child psychology in 1929, establishing there, in 1955, his International Centre of Genetic Epistemology. He remained at the University of Geneva for the rest of his life, publishing widely and gaining an international reputation for his theories on developmental psychology. Piaget died on 17 September 1980 at the age of 84.

It was at the Sorbonne that Piaget's interest in the developmental psychology of childhood really began. He became fascinated by the kinds of mistakes children made, and the thinking strategies they employed, when subjected to reading tests. Like Montessori and Steiner, Piaget believed that children develop in set stages (though like the former and unlike the latter, his belief was grounded in empirical psychological observation rather than mysticism).

Where Steiner described three distinct developmental stages, Piaget had four. He called the first the *sensorimotor stage* where, during the first two years of life, the child acquires and deploys physical skills, while at the same time learning to explore and understand the boundaries between itself and other physical entities. The second, *preoperational stage*, occurs between the ages of 2 and 6 or 7. This is the time when thought and language develop so that the child is able to engage symbolically and representationally with the world. During the *concrete operational stage* – from around the age of 7 to 11 or 12 – the child develops conceptual and logical thought. The final stage is that of *formal operations* which lasts from about the age of 12 into adulthood. This is when human beings master complex cognitive skills such as the ability to speculate, hypothesize or infer.

Like so many other innovative educators of his day, Piaget challenged radically the idea that learners are 'empty vessels' waiting passively to be filled with knowledge. He demonstrated that learning is an active process. By speculating, hypothesizing, experimenting and making mistakes, active learners demonstrate the ability, not only to 'assimilate' new knowledge, but also to 'accommodate' radical changes in the way thought itself is organized.

Further reading about Piaget
Boden, M. A. (1979) *Piaget*. London: Fontana Paperbacks.

Plato (c.428–347BC)
The most famous and most studied of the philosophers of ancient Greece. Under the influence of Socrates (470–399 BC) rather than follow a career in politics as might have been expected of an Athenian and the son of a noble family, he turned his talents to philosophy. In the aftermath of Socrates's death in 399 BC he went travelling, returning to Athens to set up his *Academy* around about 387 BC. He spent almost all the remainder of his life at the Academy until his death in 347 BC.

A. N. Whitehead said something to the effect that the whole of Western philosophy was a footnote to Plato. At one level, of course, this is a huge exaggeration but at another level it is a tribute to Plato's influence on the philosophical agenda of Western philosophy ever since.

His most famous contribution to philosophy is his Theory of the Forms. Put very crudely indeed, this theory suggested that it was only of the forms we could have knowledge, there existed for every concept some perfect supersensible instance to which the concept referred – justice, good, chair, dog, etc. – and that everything in this world with which we are familiar is as it is because to some degree, however imperfectly, it represents, is a copy of, participates in, its appropriate form. In Plato's hands his theory of forms was a very fertile philosophical tool. *The Republic* (a dialogue of his so-called middle period) portrays an image of the just state. The just state is distinguished by the harmony of its parts. There are three groups in the Republic: the Rulers (the philosopher kings), the auxiliaries, and the rest. In other parlance, he talks of the people of gold, of silver, and of brass. Education has a key role to play in the training of its members for their appropriate role in the Republic. There is an educational regime particularly suited to the kind of individual a person is. The state is wise if it is ruled wisely by the wise. Those who by temperament and intellect are fit to be the rulers enjoy an education increasingly abstract in nature. In the early stages arithmetic, harmonics, geometry, astronomy form the stuff of the curriculum. The final stage is the study of dialectic which leads to an appreciation of the ultimate form, that of the Good. In the apprehension of the Good is to be found all that which is necessary to rule wisely. Other groups in society have an education fitted to their nature and their forthcoming role in society. Not only does this education programme bring about harmony at the societal level – each knowing its place and fulfilling its designated role – it also ensures psychical harmony in the individuals so educated – reason, spirit and appetite co-exist happily.

Only a study of Plato on education can do justice to the power of his thought. Suffice to say the Platonic emphasis upon the importance of pure thought and the power of abstract thought has influenced educational thinking and practice down to the present day. It is easy to see that the idea that the kind of education an individual enjoys is down to the kind of person he or she is does not recommend itself to those of a more egalitarian turn of mind. It is difficult to believe that Plato would have applauded the comprehensive principle. One suspects he would have deplored the abolition of the grammar schools.

Jean Jacques Rousseau (1712–1778)

Rousseau is an absolutely pivotal figure in the history of educational thought. His contribution to political philosophy is immense. As far as education is concerned, it is no exaggeration to say that we live in the post-Rousseauan world. He was born in Geneva but spent twenty years of his adult life in Paris. This period of his life had a formative influence on the direction of his intellectual interests. He got drawn into the lives of the young Parisian intelligentsia. He became particularly friendly with Diderot, a key figure in the French Enlightenment movement. Subsequent to the publication of the *Social Contract*, his great political tract and *Emile*, his seminal educational treatise, he had to flee Paris because of his religious views. His books were burnt in Geneva. After some years he was allowed to return to Paris in 1770. He continued writing, famously his rather unreliable *Confessions*, along with some indifferent plays and poems. He died in 1778.

Rousseau's vision of the education of the child is incompatible with so much of traditional education that sees the child as essentially a passive figure, following a programme of study predetermined for him or her by a teacher on the basis of considerations that owe little, if anything, to the nature and interests of the child.

There are certain salient themes informing Rousseau's *Emile*. Rousseau demands that education should start from the premiss that a child is a child. Childhood is a stage of life in its own right.

Childhood is not an illness, the cure for which is adulthood. Children are individuals. They vary one from the other. Education needs to be individualized. For education to be successful it must address the given child and devise a programme of study fitted to that particular child.

Rousseau viewed the child as 'naturally good'. This is in stark contrast to so much opinion of the time that viewed the child as naturally bad thereby encouraging the thought that the child's will had to be brought to heel. This went along with a belief in the value of beating the evil out of the child. But Rousseau thought that in advance of contact with society the child was innocent of the propensity for evil. It is the viciousness of society that corrupts.

Rousseau saw the growth of the young person as going through distinct developmental stages. Each stage demanded its own appropriate handling. These stages of development must be reflected in the kind of education afforded.

The beginning of wisdom in promoting learning was to recognize what the child could learn, not what the teacher thought he or she ought to learn. Error is profoundly more damaging than ignorance. We should allow the child to be ignorant until the child is ready and able to learn. The actual learning, certainly in the early stages, should be based on experience rather than the book. Children should learn by discovery and from experience, not from being taught.

Emile represents a thought-experiment on Rousseau's part of the implementation of these principles in the education of the child Emile. The primary emphasis upon the learner learning rather than the teacher teaching has had a massive impact on pedagogy since. The so-called child-centred movement in education looks to Rousseau as its inspiration. The greatest of the contemporary educational theorists, John Dewey, saw himself as carrying forward the ideals of Rousseau. Whether we are so impressed when we realize what is plain – that a kind of deceit is practised upon Emile in that what Emile comes to learn is what the tutor has designed he should learn – is another matter.

Whatever our thoughts about that, *Emile* has had an immense impact upon subsequent educational practice. Truly a momentous book in educational thought.

Rudolph Steiner (1861–1925)

Rudolph Steiner was born on 25 February 1861 in Kraljevec, Croatia. His father was an Austrian railway official. Steiner studied maths, natural history and chemistry at the Technical University of Vienna between 1879 and 1883. After working for six years as a tutor, he became increasingly drawn to the study of philosophy, taking as his inspiration the natural scientific writings of Goethe. In 1902, Steiner became general secretary of the German Section of the Theosophical Society. Eleven years later, he broke away from that organization to found the Anthroposophical Society. Throughout his life, he travelled extensively, preaching his particular gospel of spiritual renewal.

On 7 September 1919, following Germany's defeat in the Great War, Steiner opened his first Free Waldorf School in Stuttgart. This was a combined, co-educational primary and secondary school, catering for 256 pupils, most of whom were the children of workers from the local Waldorf-Astoria cigarette factory. Steiner died on 30 March 1925 at Dornach near Basel, Switzerland, aged 74.

Steiner reacted against the fragmentation of knowledge and experience exacerbated by the prevailing materialism and scientific rationalism of his day by attempting to rediscover a sense of spiritual certainty which had not been seen in Europe since the Middle Ages. Steiner's concept of anthroposophy expressed itself in the belief that human beings could, by training the intellect in the practice of meditation, achieve a state of heightened consciousness which would enable the soul to transcend physical boundaries and break through to the spiritual reality beyond. Through this process, the spirituality in each human being could fuse with the spirituality of the universe in mystic union.

Steiner believed that, just as the Earth had to work through its destiny in seven planetary ages, so individual human beings had to do the same by undergoing the processes of reincarnation and karma. This belief had major implications for his philosophy of education. One of the reasons why it might engage a particular English audience is that it strikes some resonance with the ideas of the Romantic poet William Wordsworth and of his mystical predecessor, Thomas Traherne, who regarded birth as a process of descending into the sublunary world from the transcendent joy of Heaven. Where Wordsworth saw the human journey from childhood to adulthood as a painful process of spiritual decay, Steiner felt that each birth marked the next stage of a continuing pilgrimage towards enlightenment. He believed that the role of the teacher was to act as a mediator between the child and world, offering guidance as it undertook the three distinct, seven-year stages of its journey into adulthood. The trinities of head, heart and hand, will, feeling and thought, Steiner believed, could be brought into balance by a school curriculum which paid due attention to creativity, craftsmanship, spirituality and an acknowledgement of the oneness of all living things.

Further reading on Steiner
Ullrich, H. (1994) Rudolph Steiner. *Prospects: The Quarterly Review of Comparative Education*, **XXIV** 3/4, pp. 555–72.

L. S. Vygotsky (1896–1934)
Vygotsky was born in a small town in Belarus, attending university in Moscow and publishing his first book in 1925. He made a major impact on theories of learning and died at the young age of 37. He lived during the dramatic age of the Russian Revolution (1917) and it is possible that much of his very radical thinking emerged as a response to significant societal change. Vygotsky's main contribution was to develop a theory of learning that relied less on biology and more on 'the contribution of culture, social interaction and the historical dimension of mental development' (Ivic, 1994, p. 471). Vygotsky sees people as being somehow incomplete without inter-action with others. In *Thought and Language* Vygotsky argues that the role of culture is highly significant as people gain control over the environment but also are affected by external stimuli. As such we cannot simply talk of learning *per se* but rather have to judge the nature of learning in relation to the particular culture that produced it and in which it has to be applied. Culture-free tests of intelligence are thus, from this perspective, impossible, whatever the advocates of IQ tests might argue. The individual learner can develop his or her own learning by this interaction with the environment as opposed to waiting for learning to be imposed from outside or for the influence of inherited factors to be simply allowed to do their job. This is enormously powerful for those who wish to promote education. It gives a great deal of hope to those who wish to see an external agent such as school as being potentially able to promote learning. Of course, criticisms can be made. Vygotsky did not develop his ideas fully either in abstract or in relation to teaching. He seems to have a remarkably benign view of the positive potential of society upon learners. It is perhaps too simplistic if Vygotsky asserts that all human development is cultural as opposed to a more significant role for 'natural' factors. Nevertheless this hopeful positive message is significant and given that work is still taking place to translate and understand Vygotsky's ideas, there should be, at the very least, a willingness to explore further the meaning of the work for schools.

Appendix: A Very Brief History of Education in England

You will remember that we were very cautious about our list of great educators in the conclusion to the book. Similar feelings are present when we come to this list of factual information. We are sure that we have *not* achieved an effective balance between including events that were regarded as being very significant at the time they were introduced and those matters which appear with hindsight to be important. We have included more information about relatively recent times than may be justified and we have yet again failed to include a proper representation of figures and events that relate to a diverse range of communities. However, for all its faults, the following list shows what many would regard as something approaching the key dates and events. It is again for the reader to find out more about these events, to challenge their inclusion and to add more to the list. In that way we will not feel that we have insisted on some inappropriate rote-learning method so that the key facts about education can be remembered, but rather that we will have made clear that we do need to have some knowledge of what has happened in education and in society more broadly if we are to make sense of contemporary issues.

1693   John Locke: 'Some Thoughts Concerning Education.' This publication was (and is) very important for the new emphases he introduced on the rights of children, their natural development and management, and the growth of the concept of utility upon the development of the curriculum.

1762   Jean Jacques Rousseau: *Emile*. This is the classic statement about nature and education.

1780   Robert Raikes opens his first Sunday school at Gloucester. This may have been a response to an emerging industrial society, with a rapidly expanding population, in which Raikes felt the need to occupy and civilize the young.

1797   Andrew Bell: *An Experiment in Education*. Bell and Lancaster – the latter publishing *Improvements in Education* in 1803 – became known for their monitorial systems in which large classes could be taught using pupil-teachers. This system was enthusiastically supported by Jeremy Bentham and became almost 'the public face' of utilitarian philosophy.

1800   Robert Owen's experiment at New Lanark began to show the way forward from a slavish subscription to monitorialism. In *A New View of Society* (1816) the importance of environment in the learning process was greatly emphasized and influenced the subsequent education of factory children and others.

1802   Health and Morals of Apprentices Act. Religious teaching was compulsory for apprentices and reading, writing and arithmetic were to be taught for the first four years of the apprenticeship.

1810   Royal Lancastrian Society founded. This would later become the British and Foreign School Society and became very influential in establishing schools that tended not to be allied to the Church of England.

1811   National Society founded. This became a rival to the British and Foreign School Society. The National Society was Anglican.

1820   The foundation of London University. During the nineteenth century, university reform is very significant and important for understanding later developments. London University was influential in the development of provincial university colleges.

1828   Thomas Arnold becomes Head of Rugby School. A number of famous individuals are recognized as pioneering head teachers of public schools at this time.

1832   Parliamentary Reform Act. More men are now allowed to vote. The number of people eligible to vote would become an important factor in the growth of state education. Voters need to be able to read and write and understand at least some aspects of society.

1833   Factory Act. Children working in factories were to have two hours' teaching each day. A government grant of £20,000 was given to build 'school houses'.

1850   Frances Buss founded the North London Collegiate School. This is regarded as an important step in the education of girls.

1851   School of Mines founded. This perhaps reflects a connection between industry and education. Some argue that the perceived need for education grows along with the demands of an industrial economy.

1857   *Tom Brown's Schooldays* published. This is a famous account of life in a rather cruel private school.

1858   Dorothea Beale becomes head of Cheltenham Ladies College. There are a number of pioneering head teachers in the nineteenth century. As well as Beale, we should also include figures such as Frances Buss.

1861   The Report of the Newcastle Commission on Popular Education in England. The commission suggested that elementary schools should receive two kinds of grant. The state gave money to schools based on attendance figures. There was also money available raised through local taxation distributed to schools on the basis of payment by results. This was developed in the 1862 Revised Code so that the money came from central government. The Revised Code made clear standards of education that should be reached by children at specific ages. Payment by results was seen as the main process for improving both the level and quality of schooling. A key figure in these developments was Robert Lowe.

1864   The Report of the Clarendon Commission. This report focused on the principal public (i.e. private) schools (e.g. Eton, Winchester, Rugby). The power of the head was emphasized. The curriculum was to cover a number of areas but the classical languages and literature were seen as being particularly significant.

1867   The Parliamentary Reform Act added a million men in the towns to the franchise.

1868   Public Schools Act. The public schools that had not been part of the work of the Clarendon Commission were now to be reformed. The main recommendations were related to the organization of a three-tier system (for pupils aged up to 18, 16 or 14) of endowed secondary schools.

1869   The Endowed Schools Act. This created a commission to reform endowed schools.

1870   Education Act. W. E. Forster, a member of Gladstone's government, is the key figure. It was assumed that the voluntary system of education was insufficient. State schools (controlled by School Boards) were to be established so as to fill the gaps in existing provision. It is sometimes wrongly assumed that this Act made education compulsory. The National Union of Elementary Teachers was established in 1870. This later became the NUT. The NAS (National Association of Schoolmasters) and UWT (Union of Women Teachers) broke away in the early twentieth century.

1875   The Devonshire Report. One of the key conclusions was that science education was inadequate.

1876   Education Act (The Sandon Act). Parents were now required to ensure that their children received a proper education. Children under 10 were not to be allowed to enter full time paid employment. School attendance was to be more closely monitored.

1880   Education Act (The Mundella Act). Compulsory education was now required for children aged 5 to 10.

1884   Parliamentary Reform Act. More than a million additional men in the countryside were now eligible to vote. In this same year the Samuelson Report emphasized the importance of technical education.

1891   Elementary education was made free.

1899   School leaving age raised to 12.

1902   Education Act. This Act arose partly from the recommendations of the Cross Commission (1886–1888). Cross had attempted to rectify the financial underfunding of denominational schools by making them eligible for rate-aid. Following the 1902 Act secondary schools were now seen as a concern for the state. The School Boards were abolished and their responsibilities handed over to County and County Borough Councils. Local Education Authorities now had significant powers.

1904   A list of subjects were proposed. Elementary pupils were to study English, Arithmetic, Geography, History, Physical Exercise, Drawing for boys as well as Needlework for girls together with one or more from a list that could be taken if approved by an Inspector. Some have compared this code with the National Curriculum.

1906   Parliament encourages the provision of school meals.

1907   Medical examinations made compulsory in elementary schools. This shows that education is both part of the emerging welfare state and could be used for services to be channelled to young people.

1907   Secondary schools that received public grants now had to make a quarter of their places available to able children from elementary schools.

1918   Education Act (The Fisher Act). School leaving age raised to 14. The employment of school-age children was severely restricted. Medical examinations to take place in secondary schools. The right to vote was granted to women over 30 who were householders or wives of householders.

1926   The Hadow Report. This recommended secondary education for all. Children would attend separate primary and secondary schools. There would be grammar or senior elementary schools for those aged 11 and over. The reorganization was mostly complete by the time World War Two started in 1939.

1928   The Parliamentary Reform Act. Women were now allowed to vote as soon as they became 21. The same rule applied to men.

1939–1945   There was significant disruption caused by World War Two. Previous conflicts had not had such a severe impact. Widespread bombing and evacuation severely disrupted schooling.

1941   School milk was provided for all children at a subsidized price or free if necessary. All children received one-third of a pint of milk free. (It was restricted to primary schools in 1968 and to infants aged 5–7 in 1971.)

1942   The Beveridge Report. This is seen as the cornerstone of the welfare state. All the various schemes to support those in need were to be regularized. Beveridge was determined to attack the '5 giants': want, disease, squalor, idleness and ignorance. For the last it was felt that 'more and better schools' were needed.

1944   Education Act (The Butler Act). Most of the recommendations of the Hadow Report were to be accepted. Fee-paying grammar schools were to be mostly abolished. There would now be three stages: primary, secondary and further. The school leaving age was to be raised to 15 (this was achieved in 1947). Local education authorities were to provide schools for children according to their age, ability and aptitude. The 11-plus examination would help decide if a child was seen to be in need of an academic education (at a grammar school), a technical education or a general education (at a secondary modern school).

1951   The General Certificate of Education (GCE) in separate subjects was introduced for the most able pupils. (It replaced the old School Certificate which had been awarded if a number of passes in different subjects were achieved.)

1959   The Crowther Report. This report highlighted the wastage of talent when largely working-class children left school at the age of 15.

1963   The Robbins Report paved the way to the expansion of higher education.

1965   Circular 10/65 was issued which encouraged local education authorities to reorganize schools into a comprehensive system. The tripartite structure of grammar, technical and secondary modern schools was to be replaced by a single school for all pupils. The Certificate of Secondary Education (CSE) was introduced for the majority of pupils at 16.

1967   Children and their Primary Schools (The Plowden Report). This has been seen by some as a classic statement on the need for child-centred education.

1973   The school leaving age was raised to 16. (A decision had been taken about this in 1964.)

1976   Callaghan's 'Ruskin Speech' in which he criticizes schools for not doing enough, particularly for preparing pupils for employment.

1979   Conservative Government elected with Mrs Thatcher as Prime Minister (The Conservative Governments are in office until 1997. Mrs Thatcher was replaced as Prime Minister by John Major in 1990.)

1981   A Department for Education and Science circular required all local education authorities to produce a curriculum policy statement. Some have seen this as evidence of increasing central control of schools.

1982 Mathematics Counts: report of the committee of enquiry into the teaching of mathematics (The Cockcroft Report).

1986 The National Council for Vocational Qualifications established. Attention to vocational education is emphasized.

1988 The Education Reform Act introduces the National Curriculum. The first General Certificate of Secondary Education (GCSE) examinations. GCSE replaced GCE 'O' levels and CSE. In the GCSE examinations there was a clearer attempt to assess pupils against specific criteria. A raft of other reforms were also introduced at this time, including the right of schools to opt out of local authority control. (The Inner London Education Authority – ILEA – had already been abolished in 1988.)

1992 *Curriculum Organisation and Classroom Practice in Primary Schools* published. This report advocates a return to whole-class teaching and subject specialisms and seemed to suggest a dramatically different interpretation from that offered by the Plowden Report about what primary schools should be doing. Ofsted (Office for Standards in Education) was set up to provide inspection of schools and is seen at least in its early years, under the leadership of Chris Woodhead, as a radical force that is critical of teachers and of standards.

1995 Department for Education merges with the Department for Employment to become the Department for Education and Employment (DfEE).

1997 Labour Government elected. The National Vocational Qualifications Council merges with the Schools Curriculum and Assessment Authority to form The Qualifications and Curriculum Authority. QCA has oversight of all education, training and resultant qualifications. National Curriculum modified beginning in September 2000 for all subjects, and citizenship education to be introduced as a new subject from September 2002. A new form of AS (advanced supplementary) level examination (to be taken as a precursor to A (advanced) levels) in an attempt to broaden the curriculum followed by post-16 students.

2001 Labour re-elected. Further attention given to specialist schools (those that would deliver the National Curriculum but also specialize in a particular area such as arts, technology, sport) in an effort to 'modernize' the comprehensive education system. Increasing attention given to debates about the influence of private enterprises in schools. The DfEE becomes the Department for Education and Skills (DfES).

References

Abraham, J. (1995) *Divide and School: Gender and Class Dynamics in Comprehensive Education*. London: Falmer Press.

Althusser, L. (1972a) Ideology and Ideological State Apparatuses. In B. R. Cosin (ed.) *Education: Structure and Society* (pp. 242–80). Harmondsworth: Penguin Books.

Althusser, L. (1972b) *Lenin and Philosophy and Other Essays*. London: New Left Books.

Appleby, J., Hunt, L. and Jacob, M. (1994) *Telling the Truth About History*. New York: Norton.

Atkinson, J. (1995) The Teaching of Literature. In R. Protherough and P. King (eds) *The Challenge of the National Curriculum*. London: Routledge.

Barnett, C. (1986) *The Audit of War*. London: Macmillan.

Bates, I., Clarke, J., Cohen, P., Finn, D., Moore, R. and Willis, P. (1984) *Schooling for the Dole*. London: Macmillan.

Baumann, A. S., Bloomfield, A. and Roughton, L. (1997) *Becoming a Secondary School Teacher*. London: Hodder & Stoughton.

Bellow, S. (2001) *Ravelstein*. London: Penguin.

Bloom, A. (1987) *The Closing of the American Mind*. New York: Simon & Schuster.

Bloom, B. S., Englehart, M. B., Furst, E. J., Hill, W. H. and Krathwohl, O. R. (1956) *Taxonomy of Educational Objectives: The*

Classification of Educational Goals. Handbook 1: The Cognitive Domain. New York: Longman.

Bolter, J. D. (1991) *Writing Space: The Computer, Hypertext, and the History of Writing.* Hillsdale, NJ: Erlbaum.

Bowles, S. (1983) Unequal Education and the Reproduction of the Social Division of Labour. In B. Cosin and M. Hales (eds) *Education, Policy and Society: Theoretical Perspectives.* London: Routledge & Kegan Paul.

Bruner, J. S. (1960) *The Process of Education.* Cambridge, Mass.: Harvard University Press.

Bruner, J. S. (1966a) *A Study of Thinking.* Chichester: Wiley.

Bruner, J. S. (1966b) *Towards a Theory of Instruction.* New York: Norton.

Bruner, J. S. (1971) The Perfectibility of Intellect. In A. Gil (ed.) *The Relevance of Education* (pp. 3–19). New York: W. W. Norton & Company.

Callaghan, J. (1976) Towards a National Debate: Text of the Prime Minister's Ruskin Speech. *Education,* 22 October, 332–3.

Canfield, J. V. and Donnell, F. H. (eds) (1964) *Readings in the Theory of Knowledge.* New York: Appleton-Century-Crofts.

Coard, B. (1971) *How the West Indian Child is Made Educationally Sub-normal in the British School System: The Scandal of the Black Child in Schools in Britain.* London: New Beacon Books.

Cobb, P. (1999) Where is the Mind? In P. Murphy (ed.) *Learners, Learning and Assessment.* London: Paul Chapman Publishing.

Cosin, B. and Hales, M. (eds) (1983) *Education, Policy and Society: Theoretical Perspectives.* London: Routledge & Kegan Paul.

Crick, B. (2000) *Essays on Citizenship.* London: Continuum.

Crick, B. and Porter, A. (1978) *Political Education and Political Literacy.* London: Longman.

Crowley, T. (1991) *Proper English? Readings in Language, History and Cultural Identity.* London: Routledge.

Dagger, R. (1997) *Civic Virtues: Rights, Citizenship and Republican Liberalism.* Oxford: Oxford University Press.

Dahl, R. A. (1982) *Dilemmas of Pluralist Democracy: Autonomy versus Control.* New Haven: Yale University Press.

Davies, I., Gregory, I. and Riley, S. C. (1999) *Good Citizenship and Educational Provision.* London: Falmer Press.

De Sola Pinto, V. and Roberts, W. (1964) (eds) The Complete Poems of D. H. Lawrence. London: Heinemann.

Dewey, J. (1916, 1966 edn) *Democracy and Education.* London: Macmillan.

Dickinson, P. (1992) *A Bone from a Dry Sea*. London: Corgi Freeway.

Dore, R. (1997) *The Diploma Disease: Education, Qualification and Development*. University of London: Institute of Education.

Douglas, J. W. B. (1964) *Home and the School*. London: MacGibbon & Kee.

Education Act 1944 (7 and 8 Geo. 6, C 31) in D. J. Beattie and P. S. Taylor. *The New Law of Education* (1944) London: Butterworth & Co.

Education (No. 2) Act 1986 (C 61) London: HMSO.

Education Reform Act 1988 (C 40) London: HMSO.

Evans, R. (1997) *In Defence of History*. London: Granta.

Evans, R., Newmann, F. and Warren Saxe, D. (1996) Defining Issues Centered-Education. In R. Evans and D. Warren Saxe (eds) *Handbook on Teaching Social Issues*. Washington: National Council for the Social Studies.

Freire, P. (1990) *Pedagogy of the Oppressed*. New York: Continuum.

Freire, P. and Macedo, D. (1987) *Literacy: Reading the Word and the World*. South Hadley, M.A.: Bergin & Garvey Publishers.

Fukuyama, F. (1992) *The End of History and the Last Man*. London: Hamish Hamilton.

Gardner, H. (1993) Frames of Mind: The Theory of Multiple Intelligences. New York: Basic Books.

Gerhart, H.-P. (1993) Paulo Freire. *Prospects: The Quarterly Review of Comparative Education*, **23**, 3&4, pp. 439–58.

Gleeson, D. (1987) *TVEI and Secondary Education: A Critical Approach*. Milton Keynes: Open University Press.

Gray, J. (1998) *False Dawn: The Delusions of Global Capitalism*. London: Granta.

Green, A. (1997) *Education, Globalization and the Nation State*. London: Croom Helm.

Hahn, C. L. (1998) *Becoming Political: Comparative Perspectives on Citizenship Education*. Albany: SUNY.

Halsey, A. H., Floud, J. and Anderson, C. A. (1961) *Education, Economy and Society*. New York: The Free Press of Glencoe.

Halstead, J. M. and Taylor, M. (2000) *The Development of Values, Attitudes and Personal Qualities: A Review of Recent Research*. Slough: National Foundation for Educational Research and University of Plymouth.

Heater, D. (1984) *Peace Through Education: The Contribution of the Council For Education in World Citizenship*. Lewes: The Falmer Press.

Heater, D. (1999) *What is Citizenship?* Cambridge: Polity Press.

Heater, D. (2000) *History of Citizenship*. Leicester: Allandale Online Publishing.

Hesse, H. (1979) *The Glass Bead Game*. Harmondsworth: Penguin.

Hicks, D. (ed.) (1988) *Education for Peace: Issues, Principles and Practice in the Classroom*. London: Routledge.

Huckle, J. (1990) Environmental Education. In B. Dufour (ed.) *The New Social Curriculum: A Guide to Cross Curricular Issues*. Cambridge: Cambridge University Press.

Hughes, R. (1993) *The Culture of Complaint*. Oxford: Oxford University Press.

Hurd, D. (1989) Freedom Will Flourish Where Citizens Accept Responsibility. *The Independent*, 13 February.

Illich, I. (1973) *Deschooling Society*. Harmondsworth: Penguin.

Isin, E. F. and Wood, P. K. (1999) *Citizenship and Identity*. London: Sage.

Ivic, I. (1994) Lev S. Vygotsky. *Prospects: The Quarterly Review of Comparative Education*, **24**, 3&4, pp. 471–85.

Jackson, B. and Marsden, D. (1966) *Education and the Working Class*. Harmondsworth: Pelican.

Jenkins, K. (1995) *On 'What is History': From Carr and Elton to Rorty and White*. London: Routledge.

Jenkins, R. (1991) *A Life at the Centre*. London: Macmillan.

Jowell, R. and Park, A. (1998) *Young People, Politics and Citizenship: A Disengaged Generation?* London: Citizenship Foundation.

Kermode, F. (1964) (ed.) *The Arden Edition of the Works of William Shakespeare: The Tempest*. London: Methuen. (All quotations from the play are taken from this edition.)

Lee, P. and Ashby, R. (2000) Progression in Historical Understanding Among Students Ages 7–14. In P. N. Staerns, P. Seixas and Sam Wineburg (eds) *Knowing Teaching and Learning History*. London: New York University Press.

Lister, I. (1973) Education, Politics and a Vision of Man: A Conversation with Paulo Freire. Draft text of an article for *The Times Higher Education Supplement*. Available from the Department of Educational Studies, University of York.

Locke, J. (1964) An Essay Concerning Human Understanding. In J. V. Canfield and F. H. Donnell, Jr. (eds) *Readings in the Theory of Knowledge* (pp. 257–60). New York: Appleton-Century-Crofts.

McLaren, P. L. and Lankshear, C. (eds) (1994) *Politics of Liberation: Paths from Freire*. London and New York: Routledge.

Macedo, D. (1994) Preface. In P. L. McLaren and C. Lankshear (eds) *Politics of Liberation: Paths from Freire*. London and New York: Routledge.

Martin, J. (1999) Gender in Education. In Matheson, D. and Grosvenor, I. (eds) *An Introduction to the Study of Education*. London: David Fulton Publishers.

Marwick, A. (2001) All Quiet on the Postmodern Front. *The Times Literary Supplement*, 23 February, p. 13.

Maslow, A. H. (1954) *Motivation and Personality*. New York: Harper & Row.

Mathieson, M. (1975) *The Preachers of Culture: A Study of English and Its Teachers*. London: George Allen & Unwin.

Matthews, G. M. (1970) (ed.) *Shelley: Poetical Works*. London: Oxford University Press.

Megill, A. (1985) *Prophets of Extremity*. Berkeley: University of California Press.

Midwinter, E. (1972) Curriculum and the EPA Community School. In R. Hooper (ed.) *The Curriculum: Context, Design and Development*. Edinburgh: Oliver and Boyd.

NCC (National Curriculum Council) (1990) *Education for Economic and Industrial Understanding*. York: NCC.

Neill, A. S. (1962) *Summerhill: A Radical Approach to Education*. London: Gollancz.

Ostriker, A. (1977) (ed) William Blake: The Complete Poems. London: Penguin.

Peters, R. S. (1966) *Ethics and Education*. London: Allen & Unwin.

Pike, G. and Selby, D. (1988) *Global Teacher, Global Learner*. London: Hodder & Stoughton.

Protherough, R. and Atkinson, J. (1991) *The Making of English Teachers*. Milton Keynes: Open University Press.

Putnam, R. D. (1999) *Bowling Alone: The Collapse and Revival of American Community*. London: Simon & Schuster.

Raine, C. (1979) *A Martian Sends a Postcard Home*. Oxford: Oxford University Press.

Reimer, E. (1971) *School is Dead: An Essay on Alternatives in Education*. Harmondsworth: Penguin.

Rey, M. (1997) Human Rights Education and Intercultural Relations: Lessons for Development Educators. In J. Lynch, C. Mogdil and S. Mogdil (eds) *Education and Development: Tradition and Innovation*. London: Cassell.

Ross, A. (2000) *Curriculum: Construction and Critique*. London: Falmer Press.

Rousseau, J. J. (1911) *Emile*. New York: Dutton.

Rowberry, G. (2000) Citizenship in Education. *Ink Pellet*, **16**, 8.

Rowe, D. (2000) Value Pluralism, Democracy and Education for Citizenship. In M. Leicester, C. Modgil and S. Falmer (eds) *Education, Culture and Values. Volume VI: Politics, Education and Citizenship* (pp. 194–201). London and New York: Falmer Press.

Rubinstein, W. D. (1993) *Capitalism, Culture and Decline in Britain 1750–1900*. London: Routledge.

Rusk, R. R. (1985) *Doctrines of the Great Educators*. London: Macmillan.

Saffange, J.-F. (1994) Alexander Sutherland Neill. *Prospects: The Quarterly Review of Comparative Education*, **24**, 1&2, pp. 217–29.

Sidgwick, H. (1868) The Theory of Classical Education. In *Essays on a Liberal Education*. London: Macmillan. Cited in Mathieson, M. (1975) *The Preachers of Culture: A Study of English and Its Teachers*. London: George Allen & Unwin.

Skeggs, B. (1997) *Formations of Class and Gender: Becoming Respectable*. London: Sage.

Slavin, R. E. (1991) *Educational Psychology: Theory into Practice*. Boston: Allyn & Bacon.

Smith, A. (1998) *Accelerated Learning in Practice: Brain-based Methods for Accelerating Motivation and Achievement*. Stafford: Network Educational Press.

Snow (1959) *The Two Cultures*. New York: Cambridge University Press.

Stradling, R. (1984) *Teaching Controversial Issues*. London: Edward Arnold.

Tate, N. (1995) How Would You Teach a Child What It Means to be English? *The Independent on Sunday*, 23 July, p. 6.

Tate, N. (1999) What is Education For? *English in Education*, **33**, 2, pp. 5–18.

Taylor Committee (1977) *A New Partnership for our Schools*. London: HMSO.

Tooley, J. (2000) *Reclaiming Education*. London: Cassell.

Trafford, B. (1997) *Participation, Power-sharing and School Improvement*. Nottingham: Educational Heretics Press.

Westbrook, R. (1993) John Dewey: *Prospects: The Quarterly Review of Comparative Education*, **23**, 1&2, pp. 277–91.

White, J. (1989) An Unconstitutional National Curriculum. In L. Bash and D. Coulby (eds) *The Education Reform Act: Competition and Control*. London: Cassell.

White, J. (2000) *Do Howard Gardner's Multiple Intelligences Add Up?* London: Institute of Education.

Index

Whitty, G. (1992) Lessons from Radical Curriculum Initiatives: Integrated Humanities and World Studies. In A. Rattansi and D. Reeder (eds) *Rethinking Radical Education: Essays in Honour of Brian Simon*. London: Lawrence & Wishart.

Whitty, G., Rowe, G. and Appleton, P. (1994) Subjects and Themes in the Secondary School Curriculum. *Research Papers in Education*, **9**, pp. 159–81.

Witkin, R. (1974) *The Intelligence of Feeling*. London: Heinemann Educational Books.

Wolfe, D. (1999) Visions of Citizenship Education. *Oxford Review of Education*, **25**, 3, pp. 425–30.

Woolf, V. (1984) *A Room of One's Own*. London: Chatto & Windus.

Young, I. M. (1992) Five Faces of Oppression. In T. E. Wartenberg (ed.) *Rethinking Power*. Albany, New York: State University of New York Press.